concepts and skills of oral communication

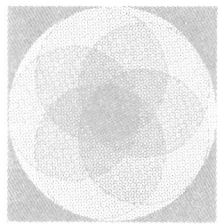

Second Edition

concepts and skills of oral communication

Dominic A. LaRusso
University of Oregon

WM. C. BROWN COMPANY PUBLISHERS, *Dubuque, Iowa*

SPEECH COMMUNICATION SERIES

Consulting Editor
Baxter M. Geeting
Sacramento State College

Copyright ©1967, 1973 by Wm. C. Brown Company Publishers

Library of Congress Catalog Card Number: 72—77976

ISBN 0—697—04114—X

All rights reserved. No part of this publication may be reproduced, stored in a retrieval system, or transmitted, in any form or by any means, electronic, mechanical, photocopying, recording, or otherwise, without the prior written permission of the copyright owner.

Second Printing, 1974

Printed in the United States of America

Dynamic developments of our time, particularly the communication explosion and new revelations concerning human behavior, demand fresh approaches to the teaching of speech. Modern life places an emphasis on speech as an *act of communication,* interdisciplinary in nature, capable of adding new dimensions to man's evolution and progress in all areas of life. The SPEECH COMMUNICATION SERIES, addressed to the introductory student, represents a significant attempt to provide new materials for today's teaching needs.

Basic to all titles in the series is the desire to present the material in the clearest and most lucid style for the purpose of making speech communication a useful, ethical, and satisfying experience. While the individual titles are self-contained, collectively they provide the substance for a comprehensive study of those topics fundamental to a basic course in speech communication.

To
YOU
from
me

CONTENTS

Introduction ... ix

PART I ORAL COMMUNICATION
Proportion and Detail

Chapter

1. **Nature of Communication** ... 3
   - Nonverbal Communication ... 7
   - Verbal Communication ... 27
   - Summary ... 34
   - Practical Reminders ... 34

2. **Principles of Effective Oral Communication** ... 39
   - Principal A ... 40
   - Principal B ... 41
   - Principal C ... 42
   - Principal D ... 45
   - Summary ... 45
   - Practical Reminders ... 46

PART II ORAL COMMUNICATION
Method and Meaning

3. **Skills of the Speaker: Speaker-Listener Analysis** ... 49
   - Speaker Analysis ... 50
   - Audience Analysis ... 56
   - Summary ... 61
   - Practical Reminders ... 62

4. **Skills of the Speaker: Message Analysis** ... 67
   - Clarity ... 67
   - Development ... 70
   - Style ... 78

Summary	83
Practical Reminders	83
5. Skills of the Speaker: Situation Analysis	**88**
Summary	92
Practical Reminders	92
6. Skills of the Speaker: Delivery	**94**
Rehearsal	94
Presentation	98
Summary	107
Practical Reminders	107

PART III ORAL COMMUNICATION
Action and Reaction

7. Skills of the Listener: Preparation	**111**
Understanding the Nature of Listening	111
Adjusting to the Demands of Listening	115
Summary	117
Practical Reminders	117
8. Skills of the Listener: Participation	**119**
Effecting an Active Role	119
Summary	126
Practical Reminders	126
Index	**129**

INTRODUCTION

IMPORTANT TRIFLES

Each year hundreds of young people enter adulthood with little or no ability in the basic patterns of social living. Ironically, more money and effort are spent to repair these abilities than to teach them correctly in the first place. Somehow, within the last seventy-five years especially, the idea of learning to do things "naturally" has dominated education. The thought is that desirable habits of thinking, creating, and communicating can be acquired without expending special time, money, or effort. Actually, these are among the most unnatural acts of man in that the precise coordinations of thought, nervous and muscular reaction are too complex to be acquired by mere growth. Moreover, the demands of modern living require that these habits be refined to the utmost and one who depends upon learning them "naturally" faces serious handicaps. The natural style is as misleading as it is misunderstood.

When athletes speak of a natural style, they do not assume a person who runs, throws, jumps, or swims as he did in his childhood. They mean, instead, the well coordinated and superbly conditioned person who has disciplined his natural strength and rhythm to produce an effortless flowing pattern of movements suited for some particular sport. So, too, when professionals speak of a natural style in communication, they do not mean speech studded with grammatical inconsistencies, conceptual incongruities, contradictions, and redundancies. They refer, rather, to speech which is sensitively worded, organized, and adapted. Naturalness alone can rarely create such sophisticated patterns of behavior.

Likewise, rules alone fail to produce masterpieces. While adherence to rules will improve the artistic performance, slavish dedication to them will produce little more than mechanical imitation. Still, a sensitive understanding of successful theory is as important to a potential athlete as it is to a fledgling doctor, engineer, or teacher. All sophisticated human activity is best learned through a skillful combination of *theory, model,* and *guided practice*. Each is important in its own right, but together they serve to initiate, develop, and sustain all the worthwhile activity of civilization.

While all learning of this nature is, at first, ponderous and mechanical, it soon becomes the automatic foundation of future success in all matters from sport to intellect. The miraculous save made by a goal tender in a professional hockey game results from immediate inspiration which releases well-trained habits of the past. The good speaker is one whose spontaneous thoughts, language, and delivery result from flexibility *inspired by a thorough mastery of rules, directed by good models,* and *insured* by *guided practice*. Truly, success derives from blending nature and art.

This book strives to define the essential ingredients in successful communication. Moreover, it furnishes models and directions for rewarding practice. But the one thing it cannot provide, the one thing that furnishes the key to improvement, is *desire*. With desire, anyone can improve in anything; without it, all the theory and models available could not produce one iota of change.

In other words, improvement depends upon the consent of the learner. Such consent is reflected, in part, by the dedication and willingness of the learner to expend almost as much time and effort as that put forth by the teachers who gather the theory and invent the experiences.

PART I

ORAL COMMUNICATION
Proportion and Detail

Our Speech reveals the height, depth, and width of our lives.

"Carl Sandburg," Connecticut, 1936, Edward Steichen, Photographer
Photography Annual, 1960. Montage
Collection of the Museum of Modern Art, New York.
Used by permission.

Chapter *1*

NATURE OF COMMUNICATION

It should be commonplace that human civilization would not be possible without communication. Since societies are formed by the interaction of individuals, and since this interaction is more symbolic than physical, some system of sharing desires and fears must be part of man's civilized traditions. That system, conceived in faith and nurtured by man's strong need for companionship, is *symbolization*. It remains the greatest single achievement of mankind—atom bomb and guided missiles notwithstanding.[1]

By realizing that he remained alone unless he could translate his experiences to himself and to others, man endeavored to convert his experiences into symbols. As a result of symbolization, man for the first time could get beyond the limits of his physical being and thereby leave the animal class. In the beginning, symbols were very closely associated with the thing they represented. In written form, early symbols were actually attempts to represent objects—diagrams of men, animals, the sun, and the like. In oral form, most of the symbols were onomatopoeic (they sounded like the thing they sought to represent). Words such as *buzz, bang, boom, purr, choo-choo, and cuckoo* are examples of this early form of symbolization. Obviously, under these conditions, individual members of such primitive societies were quite limited in their ability to share experiences and desires. When the need arose for group members to interact with more precision and regularity, and when relationships had to be described or values explained, then the symbols increased in number and complexity. With this expansion in the number and complexity of the symbols, individual and group potentials were also expanded. Living conditions improved and travel increased; religion, education, and government were made possible. Ultimately, man discovered that without leaving home he could

---

1. See Ernst Cassirer, *An Essay on Man* (New Haven, Conn.: Yale University Press, 1944), Chapters II and VIII.

travel to the farthest regions of space, share the experiences of those who journey around the world, explore the innermost secrets of the atom, and reach across the centuries to share the thoughts of past leaders of our civilization. And, further, he could relive these experiences anytime he chose to do so.

The degree to which man can transcend his inherent limitations of space and time is, as mentioned earlier, directly dependent upon the nature of his particular system of symbolization.[2] As noted earlier, the number and functional complexity of the symbols reveal the nature, scope, direction, and strength of past interactions experienced by members of the society using the system. These record, also, the value system of that society, for they preserve concepts and objects which have been considered significant as they preserve and reflect their degree of importance. The Greeks have three words for *love*—most societies have only one. The Eskimo, it is said, has at least a half dozen words for *snow*, while many of the Polynesian tribes have none. Most societies can refer to the concept of *history* by using any one of several words—the Trobriander tribe does not have one. The nature of the system is such that no speech is *truly* personal. The tribal vocabulary, the rules of grammar, and the common experiences of group members combine to guide the individual's speech in a highly predictable fashion. Any use of conventional symbols carries the mark of previous order and organization which must always play its role—no matter how incidental. To know a particular system of symbolization, therefore, is to know the culture of the people who created the system. To know a system of sounds is to be able to detect within its aural anatomy the reflections of both the lights and shadows of past centuries.

But with all of its marvels, as with all things human, the process of symbolization carries within itself the seeds of its own destruction. As man began to appreciate the true value of release from the prison of his internal and external environments, he began to immortalize his liberator—the symbol. Easily misled by his desire to seek a cause for every effect, man soon believed that the symbol was, *in fact,* the very thing or function it represented. It became easy to believe that by controlling the symbol he controlled the thing itself. He believed that mere articulation of the symbol was synonymous with exerting definite and dramatic control over the person, place, or function. So, even God could be controlled (note the Commandment "Thou shalt not take the name of the Lord, thy God, in vain"); that by changing the symbols for it an unpleasant experience or a threatening force could be made less unpleasant or less threatening (note the substitution of "passed away" for "died" and "conflict" for "war"); that by assuming a title, one could assume that qualities associated with that title

---

2. *Ibid.,* pp. 29-35, 130-136.

(note such nicknames as "Dude" or "Tiger" or "Killer"). Such beliefs exist today. Because of this belief in the power of words, most societies—even in the age of missiles—still use oaths, blessings, curses, prayers, treaties, and the like.

This is not to say that man has consistently ignored the relationship between the symbol and what it represents. During Biblical times, Hebrew scholars tried to describe the nature and scope of this connection. The early Greeks pondered the problem as well. And medieval scholars gave their concern dramatic proportions by holding laborious debates over the nature of this relationship. Some declared that not only were the symbol and the referent inseparable but that the very process of thinking was made possible only by the ability to articulate symbols. So strongly did some medievalists believe this, that the habit of silent reading was discouraged in many schools and monasteries. Other medieval scholars were inclined to consider symbols as arbitrary, conventionalized patterns that were constantly subject to change. They reasoned that since every symbol is a convention or a commonly agreed upon substitute for something else, and since these agreements vary from society to society, no natural bond is in evidence. It is this school of thought which identifies the semantic approach to oral communication today.

This approach argues that within any given society the original agreements vary as the symbols are used by different individuals who are removed in time, space, or maturity from the *original act* of agreement. This distance of time and space, in addition to adding the differences of custom, manner, ideals, and general experiences which inevitably develop, tends to lessen the degree of conscious involvement. It is observed in the present day citizen who wishes to talk about alchemy or jousting or voodoo. It is epitomized by the modern student entering a building named for a distinguished person. To the student, it is just a name (which he often mispronounces) attached to a building which he uses impersonally; to the donors, it is a memory which is relived and stimulated with each encounter. Thus, every communicator must realize that the bond between symbols and objects changes from culture to culture and within cultures, changes occur from time to time and from speaker to speaker. *All that is really required is that symbols are used in accordance with certain traditions, and when they are not, both speaker and listener be made aware of the manner in which they are being used.*

The traditions surrounding every society's system of symbolization allow for both social needs and individual preferences. While the degree to which this is allowed varies from society to society, most all groups expect social usage to be in occasional competition with private usage. The more the communicators move away from a concern with the concrete and simple phenomena in the surroundings, the more definite becomes the competition. As attention turns to such functions as relationships, feelings, desires, and moods instead of objects ("love" instead of "you"), the more difficult it becomes to use symbols correctly. In other words, while the number and nature of symbols used by two individuals in a given culture can be objectively recorded the *actual meaning* cannot. Why not?

To understand another human being's involvement in the communicative act, one must seek to discover that human being's understanding of the social concept; he must determine how his companion views the bond which permits them to share the experiences of speaker-listener or writer-reader. Men speak with more than their tongues. Entire lives issue forth in the utterance of but a few sentences. Some speakers, having lived widely and experienced deeply, realize the symbols of society permit and even encourage ambiguity; other speakers do not. Certain communicators are aware of the fact that some symbols *create* a concept while others merely *represent* one (as in poetic communication, for example). Other speakers realize that one symbol may act in both capacities and, many times, most symbols do. Many look upon social meanings as static representations of traditional thoughts, passions, and actions, and move to rebel against them. As a definite blow against convention, tradition, or authority, many subgroups within a society devise their own special meanings for common symbols (note the current meanings of *camp, tough, fuzz, stud,* and so forth). During moments of military occupation, many times special meanings are constructed for common symbols in order to insure secrecy and to deal a silent blow against the convention of the moment. Thus, pinpointing even the more objective and standardized meanings of the symbols employed by a speaker in any given situation is a difficult but necessary understanding.

Moreover, to understand another man's attempt at communication, one must understand the dimensions and strength of his *private interpretation* of the social meaning attached to the symbols he employs. As noted earlier, every experience of modern man—imbedded as it is in symbolic activity—serves to modify his stockpile of traditional reactions to the symbols he uses in having and sharing these experiences. A man who has experienced the excruciating and continual stabs of osteomyelitis for twenty years interprets the word *pain* (both in speaking and hearing it) quite differently than a person who has felt nothing worse than a skinned knee. Since man continues to have experiences from the cradle to the grave, possibilities for a constant and continuing modification of personal or subjective meanings increase rather than decrease. Is it any wonder that misunderstandings are a very large part of man's daily communication?

But his knowledge and use of the symbols of his accepted language account for only part of his confused and misunderstood attempts at com-

Nature of Communication

munication. Since these same symbols may be written as well as spoken, since each form has its peculiar strengths and weaknesses, any indiscriminate use compounds the possibilities of error and inefficency. In other words, no amount of understanding regarding the nature of symbolization will replace the need for additional knowledge of the nature of communication of which the use of symbols is but one part. More specifically, the efficient communicator must have an understanding of the various factors —in addition to proper use of symbols—which make up this basic and complex human act. He must appreciate the existence of two major forms of communication for which he is responsible and from which others gain impressions of his knowledge, appreciations, and understandings; he is aware of the existence of both the shadow and substance of his communication; he recognizes that he communicates nonverbally as well as verbally.

NONVERBAL COMMUNICATION

The noted linguist, Mario Pei, commenting on the professional activity of some of his colleagues, observed that

> In their anxiety to restrict language to a pattern of sounds, too many linguists have forgotten that the sound-symbols of the spoken tongue are neither more nor less symbolical of human thought and human meaning than the various forms of activity (gestural, pictorial, ideographic, even artistic) by which men have conveyed significant messages to one another since the dawn of history.[3]

What Professor Pei sought to have recognized has since developed into a separate area of concentration called *nonverbal* communication. Quite beyond the initial definition offered by Professor Pei, the area of nonverbal communication includes those aspects of human behavior which convey meaning regardless of the lack of recognized (conventional) symbols such as words, lights, and numbers. It has been realized that before speech there was action, and behind all of the "reasoning experiences of man" there exists a whole wealth of "nonreasoning" experience which furnishes the very foundation for the later development of the mind. The nonverbal activity of man is fundamental and internal and many times, during crises, emerges to blot out the more superficial, externalized, and newly acquired verbal activity. So fundamental is the nonverbal activity to the development of man that it could well ". . . supply the world's needs for an inter-

---

3. Mario Pei, *The Story of Language* (New York: Mentor Books, 1949), p. 8. See also R. L. Birdwhistell, *Kinesics and Context* (Philadelphia: University of Pennsylvania Press, 1970), pp. 70-72; K. L. Pike, *Language in Relation to a Unified Theory of the Structure of Human Behavior* (The Hague: Mouton Co., 1966), Chapter 2; M. Polanyi, *The Tacit Dimension* (New York: Anchor Books, 1967), Chapter 1.

national common system [of communication]."[4] But the nonverbal communication spoken of here goes far beyond the commonly accepted view of facial expressions, gestures, posture, and the like. More, properly defined nonverbal communication exists as a supplement to the verbal while, at the same time, it functions quite apart from the verbal. It is the supplementary role of nonverbal communication which will occupy the major part of this discussion.

Here, nonverbal (or the more positive term "tacit") communication is meant to include the factors of *time, space, form,* and *action*. In its supplementary role, nonverbal communication serves to define the condition which Martin Buber has labeled the "between." In his own terms, Buber calls attention to the fact that successful communication (especially in the form of the ideal dialogue) depends upon the existence of a psychophysical area where true communion is effected. "On the far side of the subjective," Buber explains, "on this side of the objective, on the narrow ridge, where *I* and *Thou* meet, there is the realm of 'between.' "[5]

By way of analogy, the nonverbal factors of communication (time, space, form, and action) act in the same capacity as the electrochemical solutions which bathe the open areas between nerve ends within the human nervous system. You may recall that, contrary to popular belief, the nerve endings of the various nerves of the body do *not* come into physical contact with one another. When a nerve impulse travels along the main trunkline of a nerve and reaches the nerve ending, it will *not* automatically cross the junction (synapse) to the end of another nerve. This transfer of impulses from one nerve to another (needed to insure *all* human action from blinking to thinking) does not depend upon the strength, size, or speed of the impulse; no altering of the impulse will guarantee this "gap jump." What is indispensable to the exchange is the proper combination of electrochemicals (dopamine, noradrenaline, acetylcholine) which serve as a ferryboat to carry the impulse from the end of one nerve to the beginning of another. In a strikingly similar manner, when the symbols within the speaker (nerve *A*) reach the limits of his physical boundaries, they are not "automatically" carried over the psychophysical gap (the "between") to penetrate the boundaries of the listener (nerve *B*). Unless the conditions of the "between" are proper, the symbols (and their meanings) will not be allowed to cross that gap, and working upon the symbols themselves (making them stronger, sharper, of greater numbers) will not produce such a transfer; what is needed is a "psychic ferryboat" constructed by the proper combination of nonverbal factors. More than ghosts of the verbal symbols, these nonverbal factors operate independently of or in

---

4. *Ibid.*, p. 11. (See Figure 1.)
5. Martin Buber, *Between Man and Man* (Boston: The Macmillan Co., 1965), p. 204.

consort with the verbal to facilitate or inhibit communication. In short, efficacious use of these nonverbal or tacit factors may well be more important to successful communication than the nature of the verbal messages exchanged.

Time

Philosophically, the nonverbal factor of *Time* appears to have a universal impact upon the affairs and conditions of man. In the literature of the various societies, reference to the importance of Time is almost commonplace. It is praised as a savior and damned as a destroyer but always honored for its fundamental role in the life of Man. In his art, religion, literature, and daily affairs man seems preoccupied with manipulating time—to speed its passage, arrest its flow, make it static, or arrange for a sporadic movement. It is identified as the essence of life.

In communication, the use or misuse of Time plays an indispensable role in determining the success or failure of any given act. Those aspects most related are *order, cycle, depth,* and *rhythm. Order* is most easily identified in perceived regularity of relationships, be they among physical or psychological entities. Certain of these relationships (minutes, hours, days, weeks, years, etc.) can be "objectively" measured; others (meaning, cause and effect, brother-sister) are less susceptible to such measurement. Nevertheless, whenever the perceived relationship in any area is disturbed, the individual becomes irritable, confused, and distressed. More, as shall be discussed in some detail in Chapter 4, in the absence of any obvious order, the individual will inject his own. Any attempt to share concepts, attitudes or desires which does *not* consider the need for establishing a *mutually acceptable* order to both speaker and listener is obviously inviting failure. Not that every act of communication begins with an order acceptable to both speaker and listener. Effective sharing occurs when, in the process of communicating, such an order is realized even though it may have required some drastic reordering on the part of one or the other of the communicants. The most obvious example of the need for this kind of concern occurs, unfortunately, with great regularity in classrooms throughout the nation. Literature courses are most often organized (and presented to the student) in chronological order. One studies the literature of America by beginning in the 1700's and proceeds through the centuries until arriving at the present. Why can't the student study American literature by studying certain themes regardless of the time block? Accounts of war have been written in every age of American Literature. At a time when concern for war is high, why can't the student dip into the thoughts of those concerned with the Revolution, World War I, or Vietnam? Why can't he be allowed to read essays and letters by Samuel

Adams, the *Red Badge of Courage* by Stephen Crane, a poem called "The Blindman" by Hervey Allen, the memoirs of war correspondent Ernie Pyle, and similar materials which bridge chronology to take advantage of the *order* (in terms of immediate emotions, related concerns, etc.) most alive to the student listener? More examples drawn from other areas of life can easily be suggested by the sensitive communicator. It is enough at this point to reiterate the need for the speaker's concern for a sense of order in his communication which relates as closely as possible to the Time concept held by his listener.

Another feature of the broader category, Time, is *cycle*. Cycle refers to expected repetition of acts, events, thoughts, phenomena, and the like which furnishes the sense of stability desired by most organisms. But it is a repetition *with a touch of variety* which invites the feeling of controlled change, of gradual modification. Thus, a night *not* followed by daylight is inconceivable to most humans; yet to those living within the Arctic circle such a phenomenon occurs with enough regularity to create an *expectation of repetition* and, therefore, a cycle in their experience; so with days, seasons, biological needs, matters of motivation, and modes of reasoning. After all, reasoning by analogy or cause-to-effect or any other form could hardly be possible without the *expectation of repetition* or the belief that this situation is much like some situation which has been experienced in the past. It should be quite apparent that, in communicative endeavors, the reasoning processes which are obviously and carefully built so as to insure a measured movement from *what the listener knows* to what the speaker *wishes him to share* are founded upon the need for listeners to experience a sense of stability. The listener perceives this stability in the form of testimony, statistics, examples, and analogies which support the cyclic concept of experience; thus, facts and figures and ideas of the past recur to provide some foundation for the intellectual and emotional leaps into the future. In this vein, even the insignificant *repetition* of basic ideas *within a presentation* (main arguments with their chief supports) builds upon the need for a sense of cycle in the human personality. Perhaps the most eloquent statement of the recognition of cycle in human affairs is that offered by the unknown preacher writing in *Ecclesiastes* of the Old Testament:

> To everything there is a season,
> And a time to every purpose under the heaven;
> A time to be born, and a time to die;
> A time to plant, and a time to pluck up that
>   which has been planted;
> . . . .
> A time to weep, and a time to laugh;
> A time to mourn and a time to dance;
> . . . .

> A time to rend and a time to sew;
> A time to keep silence and a time to speak;
>
> . . . .

Related to the features of order and cycle in Time is the element of *depth*. Awareness of the past and the ability to anticipate the future mark man as strikingly different from other members of his animal world. His history (itself an indication of this "unique" sense of time) is filled with actions, events, and concepts giving testimony to the notion that man *needs* to have a quality of depth to his consciousness; he *needs* to know that he (his *self*) extends beyond any given moment that he has roots (his own past plus that of his parents, etc.), and he has growing space (his future).

The intellectual heir of Grecian, Hebrew, and early Christian philosophers was St. Augustine. In his *Confessions* (Book XI, Chapter XIVff), Augustine reasoned that all normal men operated on a belief in present memory (actually the past), awareness (actually the present), and expectation (actually the future). Upon this belief one could build images of Heaven and Hell, Good and Evil, Reward and Punishment, and other concepts designed to affect the behavior of men. Upon this belief are based the actions of psychiatrists, educators, ministers, politicians, parents, and friends. In their endeavor to communicate with their neighbors, successful members of the groups listed above always weave these aspects of time (past, present, future) together carefully and purposefully. They realize that exclusive use of the past is as ineffective as exclusive concern with either the present or the future; that "normal" human beings move back and forth among these categories of Time although some amount of favor is given to the future since it permits the existence of hope and encourages the element of creativity. There should be a dynamic balance between use of facts (testimony, opinions, and statistics of *past* phenomena used as the materials of thought) and inferences (conclusions generally related to matters of value and directed toward the *future*) in any attempt to share with others.

In addition to order, cycle, and depth, Time manifests itself in *rhythm*. In point of fact, rhythm is a factor in order, cycle, and depth as they are applied to everyday situations. It is so much a part of the naturalness of man that its absence may easily result in the rejection of anything from objects to ideas which is nonrhythmical or out of phase with the individual observer. While it may not be instinctive, the sense of rhythm lies deeply embedded in the human organism as it does in his animal and plant companions. The phenomenon of daily or "*circadian*" rhythms is obvious enough to demonstrate the ". . . almost incredible capacities of animals and plants to orient and adjust their activities in terms of terrestrial time and space."[6] As a symmetrical animal with bilateral brain structures rhythmically controlling opposite sides of the body; a heart beating in rhythmical pattern (which, when interrupted, leaves the individual in a state of panic—at least); a rhythm accompanying ingestion, digestion, excretion, breathing, walking, sexual functions, and intellectual activity, it would hardly be too much to say that rhythm is fundamental to the nature of man. Yet the nature of man is inextricably tied to the nature of his environment. Internal rhythms mentioned above are affected by the external rhythms of man's environment, those which have to do with climatic conditions, planetary movements, time zones, and the like. Some evidence for this belief is being made available from recent research into what has been called the "Jet Lag phenomenon" which has been found to interfere with the important duties of diplomats who cross time zones too rapidly for the body to adjust and, consequently, find their reasoning, judgment, and general communication abilities adversely affected. Some psychiatrists believe most psychoses to be triggered by the individual's inability to adjust to space-time phenomena. It is as though "the efficiency of the time apparatus . . . becomes an index of existing efficiency of the personality as a whole."[7]

Even in this brief discussion, it should be clear that the internal and external rhythms are an indispensable part of the individual's daily experiences; perhaps not to the minute degree believed and propagandized by astrological charlatans, but enough to make professional psychiatrists, physicians, and educators sensitive to the role of rhythm in their duties. Clearly, these same rhythms must influence communication since they affect "the individual's capacity to perceive, respond and perform."[8]

Perhaps because of the rhythms so clearly evidenced in other aspects of his life, man expects—and is partial to—rhythm in his communicative experiences. Note that rhythm forms his incantations, prayers, blessings, and lullabies and, in its absence (stuttering, spastic jerking, cacophony) he is disturbed. In our native language, we tend to speak *and listen* with certain special rhythms called *phrases*—groups of words which convey agreed upon meanings. But this activity is a function of experience with the language of a given society. Newcomers to the language such as babies and foreigners undergo what has been termed true "cultural shock," largely because they focus upon single sounds and words while others about them are reacting to meaningful phrases. Until these newcomers learn the

6. F. A. Brown, Jr., "Endogenous, Biorhythmicity Reviewed with New Evidence," *Scientia*, Septième Série (1968), p. 15.
7. Ed Podolsky, "Time in Your Life," *The Psychiatric Review*, 55 (Spring, 1968), 135-141. Quote from p. 141.
8. LeRoy L. Lane, "Communicative Behavior and Biological Rhythms," *Speech Teacher*, XX (January, 1971), 16-20.

Nature of Communication

rhythms of the language, until they become familiar with matters of pausing, intonation, humor, anticipation, and similar activities, they will undergo feelings of anxiety, strangeness, and a certain degree of loneliness in the very midst of communication. It is important to realize here that this circumstance can be as true for members of a subculture (teen-agers, minority groups, senior citizens, chronically ill persons) as for obvious foreigners. Parenthetically, it may well be that *de-synchronization* (different rhythmical patterns) rather than age, nationality, color, educational level, political beliefs, or physical status is the real culprit in bad communication. Perhaps the time-honored observation that "Good speaking exists in the heart of man and bad speaking exists in space and time," is rooted in this thought. Perhaps in this thought rests the miracle which is communication —the art which overcomes space, time, and material to make *con*temporaries out of *dis*temporaries.

Effective use of rhythm assumes a recognition of the *unfolding* nature of life and all its activities. It is commonplace that, in the animal and plant worlds, we do not think of a baby or a bud as the *real* animal or plant. In our better moments, we realize that the *true* animal or plant is a collection of periods or stages, a *totality* which can be said to exist only at the time of its death. What is true of the lower animals is also true of humans. Few would deny that John at 15 is not the same John at 45, that Debbie at 18 does not think, act, or feel as Debbie at 30. No one (even the clairvoyant) has, at any point of his life, a complete, unalterable view of the future— his own or that of the world around him. In truth, of course, *we are all continuously involved in the process of becoming.* Life is continuously unfolding before us—bit by bit, not to be hastened by anyone or anything. In this fact rests the Hope of mankind, individually and collectively; in this fact rests the joy and reward of education, religion, and communication. The listener can only share the thoughts and feelings of the speaker as they are unfolded by the speaker. While the listener can (and, too frequently, *does*) anticipate, he can never *know* until the speaker unravels those thoughts and feelings. The implications are obvious enough for all who desire to improve their ability to share.

If, in fact, this *unfolding* process is common to life and, therefore, common to all participants in the communicative experience, it should apply to both speaking and listening. And it does in the form of a recognized need for a rhythm of communication which allows for *growing time*. In the area of education, for example, students are kept so busy gathering or being exposed to information, they have no time left to think about it, play with it, make valuable associations between and among the various bits stored away. "Soaking time" or that required to convert cucumbers into pickles (and students into scholars or boys into men of wisdom) is a missing ingredient in the schedules of bad teachers, bad lovers, and bad communicators in general. All this in the face of much historical testimony which supports the need for such "soaking time." Most familiar is the religious experience of meditation—the felt need for the retreats of Buddha, Moses, and Jesus, and the meditative periods of priests, monks, ministers, and rabbis.[9] The traditional sabbatical of the educator is in the same spirit as is the vacation period of Everyman. These necessary rhythms of action-contemplation, work-rest, gathering-judging, analysis-synthesis translate themselves into the needed pausing-phrasing, question-answer, assertion-support rhythms of effective communication. It is better, in other words, to understand the communicative experience as an ocean composed of ebbs and tides, undertows and wave actions which are defined by the rhythms of speaker-listener than to think of it as an abstract, single dimension model showing sender and receiver affected only by the well-regulated, sequential, and linear impulses of the message.

Thus, the nonverbal (tacit) component of Time is important because it is the framework within which communication occurs and is, itself, a factor in the sharing of meanings. It is reflected in the order or organization of our communication, in the notions of explanation and argumentation which are built upon the systematic movement from known to unknown, in our use of linguistic order and tense, in our rate of utterance and the rhythm with which we move from thought to thought and mood to mood.

Space

Anyone attempting to speak of space without reference to time (or vice versa) is struck immediately by the obviously heavy interdependence of the two. Immanuel Kant, the immortal German philosopher of the 1700s, thought of all experiences which occur outside of himself as constituting *Space* and all inner experiences as a form of *Time*. A few centuries before Kant, Renaissance philosophers emphasized a spatial aspect of knowledge with the mind acting as a great transformer converting material elements of the universal to nonmaterial so they could be handled by the individual organism. The ancient Greeks, much in the fashion of the more modern Albert Einstein, conceived of a space-time continuum wherein all the senses of man operate simultaneously. It was this tradition of thought regarding the undeniable marriage of space-time which encouraged man to undertake the explorations into both the outer spaces and the inner places of his world. More importantly, it is this tradition which underscores his

---

9. Interestingly enough, evidence is mounting regarding the beneficial reduction of certain chemical stress substances found in the blood after periods of meditation. See Nigel Calder, *The Mind of Man* (New York: Viking Press, 1970), pp. 81-95, and the popular report in *Signature* (July, 1971), p. 18.

Nature of Communication 15

heavy dependence upon communication, the art which allows him to transcend his spatial-temporal limits.

Insofar as space can be viewed at all, it appears to the perceiving human being as either *physical* or *abstract*. Physical space perception is an inherent ability of all normal newborn animals—including the human child who comes upon this ability a bit later in his development. Without great difficulty, each individual is soon able to distinguish between himself (his body) and the limits of other things. Very soon, his behavior patterns are shaped with the nature of his spatial world in mind. Someone born and raised in a city will obviously demonstrate certain behavior traits which differ from those developed by his cousin or friend who was born and raised on the plains of eastern Montana; the child of Polynesian parents in Tahiti will show certain adeptness in water and mountain skills not shown by the youngster of Arabic parents living in the Sahara desert. Even more to the point, however, is the fact that these youngsters gain impressions, appreciations, and attitudes of space along with their motor skills. In addition to being able to swim, the Polynesian child usually gathers impressions of space which might well include categories like limitless, flexible, uncontrolled, variable; he might even appreciate that his spatial environment (in part, at least) is a source of pleasure, food, transportation, and mysticism; he will almost certainly develop attitudes regarding the universal need for water, the ever-present dangers mingling with the obvious pleasures, and so forth. In sum, the human organism is affected by his physical environment *and the images he derives from that environment.*

It is this latter aspect of human behavior which is important to our discussion of the role of nonverbal factors in communication since it is man's *image* (concept) of space which plays a more frequent and telling role in shaping that behavior. Clearly, one is not always at liberty to alter the environment in order to alter the behavior of persons within that environment. Time, money, and effort often make it impossible to construct parks out of ghettos, convert arid lands into bountiful valleys, or mould an Olympic champion out of a paralyzed human body. But, in each case, the concepts related to these environments *can* be altered—an assertion supported daily by the work of friends, parents, psychiatrists, teachers, doctors, lawyers, and the men and women of religion. From this seemingly small step (advancing from the limits of the "real" environment to the symbolic manipulation of it), man derives his ability to handle concepts of *abstract space* without losing his appreciation for the more concrete images.

In its simplest form, *abstract* space is seen in the form of numbers, geometric designs, and pictorial representations such as maps, flow charts, organizational charts, and the like. More than a simple *re*-presentation of physical space, the concept of abstract space allowed man to use spatial qualities and attributes when dealing with more nonphysical materials. Thus, he began to speak of *social distance, psychic expansion, tight* or *loose reasoning, spiritual dominion*—just to name a few examples. This shift, this growth of a *consciousness of space* (thought by some philosophers to be *the* pivotal point in the "modernization" of man), made its most telling impact in the area of intellectual development. Man began to view knowledge as composed of bits of space (images) to be moved about and the mind as a storehouse in which spaces were to be filled, ordered, and modified. To this day, the ability to think is presumed to rest in one's power to introduce different images or to rearrange the relationships among the existing ones. The ability to reason is believed to improve as one becomes more and more able to locate and identify the images of knowledge, store these images, and assemble or reassemble them into some sort of meaningful pattern whenever the occasion demands. It would seem clear from this discussion that anyone failing to consider the "spatial biases" of his fellows while endeavoring to communicate with them merely increases his chances of failure.

Some of these "biases" have individual twists to them, but most all are formed by the culture (psychosocio-physical environment) within which the individual operates. Of those which have the most direct bearing upon the act of communication, *personal* and *public* space deserve attention at this point.

By *personal* space is meant everything from the individual's "bag of skin" to the abstract concepts contained within. More important than the verbal message, at times, is the metamessage delivered by the communicator's use of personal space. It is now pretty generally accepted that the human being carries with him a feeling that he is enclosed in a psychic bubble which extends beyond his physical body. This "personal bubble" extends for approximately two and one-half feet beyond the outer limits of the skin. The area enclosed by this "bubble" is considered quite personal (intimate) and accessible only to very special people. While the degree of intimacy allowed varies with each culture (the area is more rigid and larger for most Anglo-Saxons than for Latins or Japanese, for example), any uninvited intrusion of this space interferes with the sharing process. Moreover, failure to consider the impact of this area upon the ultimate end of any attempt to communicate will almost certainly decrease the chances for success. An insensitive communicator who gets too close when carrying on a conversation, speaks too loudly for the distance involved, exercises rigid and prolonged eye contact is bound to have his message (and himself) rejected. Some psychiatrists have suggested that the so-called chronic tension associated with big city living comes from the regular and frequent intrusion of this personal bubble by complete strangers over whom there is little if any control. Crowded elevators, subways, streets, apartment houses, hospitals, and even recreational areas foster a constant low-level degree of nervous-muscular "avoidance" posture which leads to the facial expressions and bodily postures so commonly associated with city dwellers, i.e., quick pace, "closed-in" or collected posture, habitual frown, pursed lips.

Beyond this more personal bubble is another area often referred to as social distance. In this area (roughly from two and one-half feet to approximately seven feet) the communicants usually share experiences which attend the business of daily living, i.e., food purchases, car repair discussions, office work. Here, too, the careful communicant works to avoid a blatant misuse of spatial forces. As the distance increases, he should find himself using more rather than less eye contact; he reserves more personal subjects (topics) for shorter distances, and ceases any attempt at sustained verbal communication when the distances get beyond ten or twelve feet except for the more formal public speaking situations.

Within this personal space area (zero to twelve feet) one can easily recognize signs of this "bias" coming into play. Note, for example, the relative ease with which one discusses the public parts of his body (head, limbs, heart, etc.) as opposed to the private parts (genital organs). Consider the seating patterns purposely chosen by friends, strangers, and enemies, teachers, psychiatrists, counselors, diplomats, labor mediators, etc. From the use of space alone, the average person is likely to assume the existence of certain social relations between two communicants whom he can see but cannot hear. Given a free choice are friends likely to sit side-by-side or one behind the other in movies, concerts, classes, churches, and so forth? When a member of a family or familiar group enters a room where other members are present and chooses a seat fifteen or twenty feet from the others, what possible metamessages is he offering? While the assumed relations drawn from these observations of the use of personal space are not always correct, the important thing to remember is that *the human tendency to draw such conclusions exists.* The effective communicator, therefore, considers his use of personal space at least as frequently as he considers his vocabulary.

This is also true of what has been termed *public* space. By public space is meant that area extending beyond the twelve feet which arbitrarily limits *personal* space. It is the area within which a person lives, works, plays, and interacts with people and things *on a more general* basis. Within this area, he is exposed to many more stimuli than involved in his personal space but in such impersonal fashion as to allow greater choice in deciding which of these will affect him. It is the area of homes, shops, offices, schools, hospitals, city streets, and legislative assemblies.

There is an observation, attributed to Winston Churchill, which introduces part of the thesis underlying the rest of this section: "First we shape our buildings, then our buildings shape us." If we interpret "buildings" to mean open areas as well as the rooms or cubicles within certain structures, then the significance of public space becomes more apparent. Where a town or city is built determines, in large part, how it will be built (street shapes, directions, distances) and how the people residing there will act. The citizens of Tukwila have habits of living which differ from those of the inhabitants of the Swiss village called Milch se Fruct—and not simply because the culture differs. The buses and automobiles which travel the wide clear streets and park in front of the low, rambling, flat-roofed houses of Tukwila, Washington, are not seen in the Swiss village of Milch se Fruct despite the fact that the populations are very similar in number. The narrow dirt paths and stoned lanes of the Swiss village encourage more bicycle and foot movement between and around the stone, compact, slant-roofed homes. Habits and attitudes about closeness and time and organization, influenced by these larger spatial considerations, soon reflect themselves in all patterns of interaction—especially communication. Where meetings are held, how often, upon what subjects, and with how many people are questions whose answers are affected by the type of spatial considerations suggested above. One can tell something of the socioeconomic atmosphere of a city by noting its spatial configuration—a fact supporting the endeavors of urban renewal projects and the dreams of most modern architects. So, too, the spaces *within* various structures begin to direct the action patterns of humans. Note the traffic flow inside schools, hospitals, and community halls; study the traffic patterns within private homes. Are "private" areas distinguished from the more public ones? How? Do certain "open" spaces located in hotels, hospitals, or private homes convey a metamessage different from spaces blocked off by doors, planters, half-partitions, and furniture? What is there about a kitchen in the home of farmers or immigrant families which acts as a magnet for friendly conversation while the parlor or living room is reserved for more formal discussions between slight acquaintances?

At least one social scientist has dedicated an entire work to the concerns of space because of the belief that:

> Knowledge about man's immediate environment, the hollows within his shelters that he calls offices, classrooms, corridors, and hospital wards, is as important as knowledge about outer space and undersea life. For too long we have accepted physical forms and administrative arrangements based upon outdated views of human activity.[10]

10. Robert Sommer, *Personal Space* (Englewood Cliffs, N. J.: Prentice-Hall, Inc., 1969), p. vii.

Our present concern focuses upon the images drawn of the communicator and/or his message as a result of that communicator's use of public space. There is an abundance of evidence to support the contention that *where* one confronts a communicative venture is as telling to the final outcome as on *what subject* and *from whom*. Obviously, in the very informal instances, a judgment is made quite rapidly without elaborate preparation and analysis. Nevertheless, even under these conditions the communicator (lover, friend, parent, teacher, or doctor) must decide the appropriateness of the subject in view of the available time and the nature of the physical location. Are not people inclined to communicate more freely and at greater length when time and place seem more appropriate? Do these factors add or detract from the impact of a message containing news of death? A wedding? A birth? A termination of a job? A transfer? A failure? Very often, too often, the communicator contradicts or compromises the act of sharing by offering it in an atmosphere which carries an impression of carelessness, friction, insincerity, and indifference, which the listener correctly reads as a *true* representation of the speaker's thoughts and feelings.

Despite the magnitude of the daily human tragedies witnessed during the Vietnamese War, international attention was focused upon an argument between Allied and North Vietnam diplomats which centered about the *shape of the table to be used for peace talks*. Fifteen years earlier, in North Korea, representatives of the United States debated with delegates from North Korea over *precisely the same issue*. Some *thirteen centuries earlier than that,* King Arthur defied tradition with his decree formulating the Knights of the Round Table. Although separated by centuries and a myriad of cultural variations, these individuals shared the realization that a *round table bespoke of equality*. Since there is no head or foot to a round table (or to a circle of chairs without a table), sensitive negotiators—whether political, industrial, educational, or social—have used such spatial relations to communicate the metamessage of care and concern for the dignity of the communicants. Even to enumerate the most important relevant examples drawn from the areas of religion, education, business, psychiatry, or family living would require another volume equivalent to this one. Enough to say at this point that traditions such as *Daddy's chair, family rooms, hobby areas, private offices, desk space and location, executive lavatories and dining rooms, counseling rooms, teacher space, pupil space, production areas, meditation spots in larger chapels, convalescent places, interior decoration, and landscape gardening* (and the considerations of color, rhythm, and textures which attend each of the foregoing examples) all bear witness to the deep-seated "spatial biases" which exist within human cultures and which must be scrutinized by every concerned communicator.

Form

When it was suggested, at the beginning of this section, that *form* played a role as a nonverbal factor in communication, one hope was that at least a vague feeling about the impact of form on living organisms would be established. As you may remember, the word *information* (from the Latin verb *informare*) means to assign form to something—anything. It has come to mean, mostly, thoughts or feelings which have been put into some arrangement easily identified by anyone other than the original form giver. Thus, what babbles issue forth from a month-old baby's mouth are not considered to be information because the *form* is not generally recognized. The sounds, words, phrases, or sentences of his soon-to-be-acquired native language are not yet evident. Yet, a trained pediatrician can often gather meaning from such "unintelligible" symbols since he is aware of a possible *form* or *order* other than those associated with language. He may note an order which reveals a relationship between the baby's internal state and his outward condition. Such an order may well alert the doctor to the difference among sounds of terror, joy, or experimentation. In the same way, we learn to distinguish between matters of *form* and *content* in all phases of life, from literature to loving and from politics to play. None of these is a product of random, isolated or sporadic activity. A form or order is imposed as a consequence of what may be a basic physiologic need for the human to free himself from chaos. Whatever its derivation, this "forming" tendency of man is reflected in all of his work and can be seen most easily in his thought, action, and expression.

Out of the chaos of experience, man seeks to identify categories which enable him to order and arrange and, in this way, demonstrate some measure of control. The salient categorizing effort of man, of course, has been his process of symbolization. From this habit of "giving form to his experiences," man moved to the incredibly complex situation of "giving experience to his forms" as represented by the activities of mathematicians, symbolic logicians, psycholinguists, and others who spend time defining relationships between symbols. So basic is this "forming tendency" of man that philosophers from Plato to Marshall McLuhan have tried to explain its nature and causation in order to harness its powers to provide clearer, sharper, and more penetrating thought processes.

Others, philosophers included, have spent an equal amount of time trying to relate form and action. Obvious examples can be drawn from the work of the physiologist, the practicing physician, or the athletic coach. Less obvious is the concern of the teacher, social workers, psychiatrist, or lawyer. Each of these professionals is concerned with *style* or form of the activity whether it be on the playing field, on the street, or in the classroom; whether it be on a microscopic scale or in a real life situation; whether in sickness or in health. In each of these cases, the concern is with giving some acceptable *form* to the random activity of the untrained and reducing or eliminating actions which interfere with the attainment of the desired or ultimate form. Thus, the undifferentiated and confused form of the amateur is gradually refined to become the smooth, effortless, and rhythmic style of the professional, be he ballplayer, surgeon, or citizen.

More than any area, however, communication feels the indispensable quality of man's ability *to form* and *to infuse form* into his experiences. Since it is dependent upon both the thought and action of man, the communicative experience is interlaced throughout his own *con-for-mation*. To shape his thought and correct his action, man is required to work with such forms as sounds, words, phrases, sentences, and actions which serve as parts of other forms called questions, oaths, prayers, arguments, propositions, or theories. Together, these forms become part of still larger forms called rhetoric, poetic, or dialectic which themselves become part of still larger forms called history, religion, education, philosophy. All these, of course, become part of the ultimate form which man has called civilization.

In our study of communication, the impact of these forms must be examined together with those often considered under the category termed *media*. These would include oral modes (face-to-face, group meetings, radio, television, etc.); visual modes (pictures, lights, color arrangements, graphics, and the like); aural modes (coded sounds, music, chants, and silence); and written modes (memos, letters, books, newspapers, and all other forms of the printed word). Although there may be some question regarding the complete acceptance of Marshall McLuhan's thought that the "medium is the message," there can be little doubt that the medium is a viable factor in the total sharing experience called communication. For the true artist, whether he deals in the plastic arts or words, the medium represents a force whose resistance aids in the development of his creativity. In addition to being concerned with the nature of his audient, the communicator (in matter or words) must occasionally be alerted to the nature of what he has at his disposal. It is here that the direction and speed—yes, even degree of union—are decided. Wood offers certain directions and permits distinct ranges of speed; clay differs from wood, and both vary from metal or paint. Words allow yet another variation and they vary from metal or paint. And the difference between oral and written symbols is a miracle which cannot be denied.

While it is impossible to detail the numerous implications of choice of form upon the outcome, we can suggest how variations of form may well determine levels of agreement, intensity, and understanding in any communicative act.

Every speaker seeking to share on an interpersonal level makes a choice (most often unconscious) as to the *macroform* which the communication will take. That is, he will decide whether to speak on a face-to-face basis or in a group situation, possibly involving some aspect of mass media such as radio or television. To the twentieth-century politician, this choice cannot often be made without a great amount of forethought. In an era when there is a growing tide of resentment against depersonalization in all areas of communal living, he cannot afford to restrict his campaign efforts to radio or television or newspapers. So, too, with teachers and other professionals whose significance rests with creating meaningful behavioral changes in others. Having selected, say, the face-to-face form, the effective communicator then makes a conscious choice between monologue and dialogue as a dominant subform. Obviously, the former has strengths (conservation of time, for one) which the latter does not, and vice versa. If one wished to convey a concern for his fellow communicant, the dialogue form is preferable since it is heavily dependent upon the response time, direction, and rhythm of the listener. Habitual use of one or the other of these subforms soon establishes *a personal style of communication* which the early Greeks labeled *Dianoia*; and, even then, a man's style or form of speech was considered as much a persuasive force as the arguments he used. One easily sees evidence for this thought in many of today's politicians, labor leaders, teachers, and parents. Having developed a style under certain conditions they find it difficult to modify it under new ones. The gruff, profane, direct leader of one era will hardly become the subtle, sensitive, and flexible leader of another. Yet this habit pattern of communication will, all too often, be of greater consequence in aiding or hindering the sharing adventure than the message itself.

If, instead, the group form is selected, the sensitive speaker must still make some of these same distinctions. He must decide if his group encounter will be with or without appointed leadership; with a few or among many; formal (parliamentary procedure, symposia, debate) or less formal (problem-solving, encounter sessions); with or without the services of such mass media as radio and television.

Pursuing the principle further, a case can be made for the intelligent choice among the various *microforms* which are a part of the larger macroforms mentioned earlier. Thus, whether in face-to-face situations or in group activity, the communicator's *rhetorical order* (the selection and organization of his words, sentences, and arguments) is important. When Chaim Perelman, in his chapter entitled "Presentation of Data and Form of the Discourse,"[11] spoke of the association between verbal forms and argumentation and, further, between form of discourse and "communion with the audience," he was making the same point. And, with little difficulty, you will find support for this thought in your own experience. Are you not "turned off" by someone who uses words improperly, badly jum-

11. Chaim Perelman and Olbrechts-Tyteca, *The New Rhetoric* (South Bend: University of Notre Dame, 1969), pp. 142-183.

Nature of Communication

bled and inappropriate to the topic or occasion? What of the speaker who uses very few transitions to help guide his listener? Do you react differently to a speaker who "builds to a climax" as opposed to one who "lays it on the line, point for point"?

From Aristotle to Pope Pius II to Kenneth Burke, it has been recognized that the very form of the concepts (declarative, interrogative, imperative, petitioning, metaphorical, repetitive, satirical, etc.) does much to enhance or minimize the communion between speaker and listener. Into this already complex condition, one could place for consideration the matter of *silence*.

In speech, one has the product of all the past agreements of his society; in silence, one finds the desert of communal experience. Silence forms the basic material out of which speech erupts; it is the warp which gives identity to the woof of communication. As with sound, all instances of silence are not equal and therefore convey different meanings. As there is meaningless speech, there exists meaningful silence. A teacher's silence following a student question obviously asked in jest may well be crushing. That same teacher's silence following a student's bona fide request for elaboration or clarification may well be complimentary. Used wisely, silence can serve as an incubator for the maturation of another's intellect and soul. Improperly applied, it can smother the delicate seeds of intellectual and emotional experimentation so necessary to the mental health of civilization. In the human condition, which appears defined by an intense and universal need to interact via oral communication, unexplained or misunderstood silence is generally considered an enemy of grand proportions. What else lies behind the great and continuing argument for freedom of speech? In the twentieth century, should we argue for a freedom of silence?

Action

Thus far, the principal aim of this section is to challenge some commonly-held notions regarding the nature of communication. At this point, the challenge is crystallized into this thesis: *We have too easily accepted the notion that the success of any communicative act is rooted in verbal activity.* Currently, there is little, if any, evidence to indicate which part of a *total* communicative act (verbal plus nonverbal) is *the* effective portion. Who is there to deny that true communication may occur *despite* (not because of) verbal activity? More and more social scientists, philosophers, and educators are of the belief that the nonverbal factor of *action* precedes and supports verbal activity.[12] Beneath the thousands of languages now being spoken on earth, if these people are correct, runs a more universal

---

12. Such men include Plato, Cicero, Leon Battista Alberti, Noam Chomsky, Jerome Bruner, Abraham Maslow and Michael Polanyi—just to name a few.

language called *action*. For, in its true universality, action is the language of no one but acts as the voice of all—prince and pauper, thief and cleric, babe and man, eagle and minnow, ant and sloth, redwood and sea. No bush or tree or animal could survive without it, and all are made better for it.

To say this is not to say that the phenomenon of action is thoroughly understood. There is much to discover and much more to understand. However, it can be said that men have long shared some measure of understanding regarding the role of action in their lives. From time immemorial, we have sought to take the measure of the *inner* man by using as a gauge his outer manner. And more, he has operated on a bit of tribal knowledge (*isomorphism*) which enables him to assume that any *perceived similarity in form, structure, or spirit* allows for a sharing experience. Thus, in primitive men and young children there exists an early fear or distrust of things which are not similar to themselves in form, structure, or spirit. As the individual matures, the distrust shrinks (or becomes refined?) and is made to include a rejection of those *humans* who differ in speech, skin color, spiritual beliefs, etc. In its positive form, this isomorphic tendency is at the base of man's ability to identify with others; it is the heart of empathy (see Chapter 6) and the spirit of education, religion, law, and medicine. Indeed, it is the foundation of all communal living.

Whether in himself or in others, the average individual assumes physical action to be the result of a coordinated effort between mind and body (psychosoma). With this thought as a basis, he uses physical action as an index to the health, motivation, and beliefs of others. Popular magazines now speak quasi-authoritatively about "body language," the theatre has seen a resurgence of the "method acting" theories of Constantin Stanislavsky, and medical practitioners have officially recognized psychosomatic medicine as a legitimate realm of endeavor. Certain interests in the field of communication have coined such words as *kinesics* (specialized actions used for purposes of communication), *mimetics* (specialized animal activity used for the purpose of survival), and *proxemics* (specialized human activity used for interaction) in order to categorize samples of this mind-body phenomenon for better analysis.

On a more practical level, an acceptance of the psychosoma tenet has led man to focus upon matters of posture, gesture, and movement in the belief that they will help him to chart the depth and range of the invisible part of his brother; these specialized actions, affected by heredity, culture, and immediate psychological state, are used by professional and layman alike to judge the health, motivation, and beliefs of others.

More than any other form of action, *posture* carries the strongest connotation of guilt. From early childhood, each of us has been almost harassed by admonitions regarding "correct" posture, and not without some justification. Whether walking, standing, sitting or lying down, the body is all too frequently abused, twisted, distorted into all sorts of unproductive and even ugly shapes. Not only are the abused positions harmful to the development and efficiency of our internal organs, but they also act as "signals" to our contemporaries revealing such matters as state of health, possible motivation, and nature and strength of belief. One need not be a practicing psychiatrist to recognize the postural differences between people who are happy or depressed, healthy or chronically ill, pensive or angry. Most often, the head and extremities are used for "reading" the conditions of the inner man. Tilting the head forward or backward, repeatedly shifting its position or maintaining a fixed position throughout the course of a communication invites the observer to draw from a myriad of interpretations. So with the use of the eyes. Eye contact very often precedes verbal contact (in extending recognition or an invitation over distances of twenty feet or more) and is, most certainly, an important complement to it. When one member of a communicative experience insists on wearing sunglasses throughout, or avoids the eyes of the other, or stares or constantly shifts his gaze, he is aiding his partner toward an interpretation of intent or motivation which may be quite different from that conveyed by the verbal message. Under the title of *Pupillography*, many psychologists are considering not only the matters mentioned above (and in Chapter 6), but also variations in pupil size as an index to mental health. The general thesis is that during moments of pleasure or a generally agreeable state, normal individuals show a dilation (enlarging) of the pupils; in instances of pain or displeasure or agitation, the pupils tend to contract (shrink). The implications of such research are obvious for those interested in matters of communication.

Even in the depths of their worst distortions, popular works have served to call attention to the often unintended messages carried by the postural variations of our extremities.[13] For many years, researchers have noted that persons experiencing certain mental and physical states characteristically assume discrete positions whether standing or sitting. But even without benefit of professional researchers, most individuals can distinguish the relaxed person and the tense, uncomfortable one by the position of their legs and arms.

Gesture, as a component of the nonverbal factor called action, is the most overworked and misunderstood factor in the 2500-year history of the study of oral communication in the Western world. Maligned by the misinformed of every age who regarded its study as tantamount to the study of

---

13. Julius Fast, *Body Language* (New York: M. Evans and Co., 1970).

the entire discipline of oral communication, gesture has nevertheless always been used as a barometer of internal human states. Whether of the head, torso, or extremities, the most universal focus has been upon the direction of the gesture—toward or away from the idea or the person involved in the communication. Thus, the nod or shake of the head, the wink, roll or twinkle of the eyes, shoulder hunching, hand clapping or wringing, foot shifts or taps—each read as an indication of the individual's tie to his inner environment and/or the external aspects of the sharing experience.

As a human gesture, especially, the significance of *touching* is becoming more and more apparent. Our "bag of skin" is now thought of as something more than a container for the internal organs. Called by some "the most important organ system of the body,"[14] the human skin enables man to sense more than just hot and cold, wetness or dryness, pressure, size and shape. Through the specialized gesture of touch (tactile sense), the normal individual senses the more intangible relationships of love, compassion, concern, or their opposites. Touching patterns vary from culture to culture but the importance of continuous tactile contact during the human early developmental periods does not. The absence of this contact has resulted in a tragic syndrome of fatal loneliness called *marasmus* and found most frequently among those babies abandoned during the early months of their lives. The lack of petting, stroking, hugging, kissing, and rocking somehow translates itself in the nervous system of these infants as a lack of concern and, literally, they waste away until they die. The same phenomenon was discovered among many of the prisoners of war captured by the North Korean conflict: physically sound men, feeling abandoned and hopeless, would retreat to a remote corner of the compound and will themselves to die.

Within the past two decades, the salience of touch to the maintenance of stable adult relationships becomes increasingly clear. With lovers, doctors and patients, parents and young children, and some good friends, the application of this fact is not difficult. It is only when one attempts to relate to other relationships (with strangers, etc.) that questions and hesitations arise. And, yet, it is in these very situations and relationships where one may hear the unspoken plea "If you hold me, you will heal me." That we recognize this need is attested to by many patterns which have now become custom: Handshaking, massage, pats of encouragement, formal dancing; even our obsession with vocalization is but an attempt to touch our neighbor by playing on his eardrum. What we have been telling each other is that, even as strangers, we need the reassurances offered by the gesture of touch. In this way, however cobweblike and transitory its na-

---

14. Ashley Montagu, *Touching: The Human Significance of the Skin* (New York: Columbia University Press, 1971), p. 7.

ture, unification is effected and the urgent thirst for meaningful contact quenched. In a society in which verbal communication is all too soon jaded and routine, where viable interpersonal relationships appear to be out of style, the gesture of touch can bring an accent of creativity to the interaction between men.

Finally, the most obvious component of action—*movement*—deserves some attention. Here, the thought is that direction, speed, and range of gross bodily action also serve as signs of certain mental states and dispositions. Recall your *re*action to the sudden, gross, and rapid movement toward (or away from) you of one—even a loved one—with whom you had been sharing some thoughts and feelings. Note also that the absence of movement in children is often thought to be distressing while in adults it carries a concept of respite or discipline. The walk of an adult is often described as an amble or a swagger or spastic and, if witnessed in members of certain minority groups, brings forth a free flow of interpretations regarding motivation (hostile, insolent, etc.).

At this point, the conclusion should be inescapable: verbalization is only the bright flower of oral communication. The communicative experience is a totality composed of the bits and pieces of verbal and nonverbal activity unfolding and merging into a continuous panasonic-panorama. Meaning is not attached to any single part any more than life or beauty is attached to any single part of a flower. In the words of Lao-Tzu:

> Foundation is his who can feel beyond touch,
> Harmony is his who can hear beyond sound,
> Pattern is his who can see beyond shape:
> Life is his who can tell beyond words
> Fulfillment of the unfulfilled.[15]

VERBAL COMMUNICATION

Throughout man's long and dynamic evolution, no revolution or war or natural calamity has ever reduced the importance of his verbal communication. If anything, these have served to dramatize its significance in every phase of his activity as they have served to demonstrate the indispensable role played by the oral form. While writing performs a prominent part of shaping and preserving man's heritage, while it serves as an important sign of the educated person, its indispensability cannot begin to compete with that of speaking. It is conceivable that man can go about in this world without having to read or write (over one-half of the world's population still does), but it is impossible to conceive of any society of

---

15. Lao-Tzu, *The Way of Life*, ed. Witter Brynner (New York: Capricorn Books, 1944), p. 52.

man which is without spoken forms. Of the approximately three thousand languages in the world today, only about 25% have written forms whereas 100% have oral forms. One can judge the civilization of man by the degree to which he converses. To the aborigines of Australia as well as the scholar in France, to the child in Lapland as well as the judge in Seattle, the oral mode of communication is the most important tool for personal development and social interaction. Thus, the focus of this book is the oral mode.

On September 20, 1954, during convocation ceremonies at Brown University, President A. Whitney Griswold of Yale University observed that this was a tongue-tied democracy which had all but lost the will and the skill to speak.[16] Assuming that this is an accurate appraisal of America's condition, how does one account for it? Does the fault lie with a lethargic public or with inept professionals? As in most cases, the truth probably rests somewhere in between these extremes. Without doubt, past habits of some inept professionals have encouraged a lethargic public; conversely, a public interested more in performance than principle, more in quantity than quality has given encouragement to the ever-present charlatan. As a consequence, the study of oral communication (now as at other times throughout its long history) has been conceived by many to be a study of the trivial, little more than a concentration upon style or the development of a cultured accent which is taken as the *sine qua non* of the Good Life. But even during periods of apparent decay, the serious study of oral communication has never ceased to develop wholesomely.

Today, in the midst of the decadence described by President Griswold, the study of speech with all of its ramifications is a flourishing pursuit—flourishing even by the standards of our inflationary age. There are now chairs and assistantships for speech in almost every large American university, public and private clinics for speech and hearing therapy, active national and regional professional societies, at least a dozen professional journals devoted to general and special problems in the field, and, above all, programs of research which promise to furnish a greater understanding of the intricacies of this most human form of communication.

Such research concerns itself with both the abnormal and normal aspects of oral communication. In the area of the abnormal, investigators are seeking, among other things, to discover significant relationships between certain environmental factors and a child's tendency to stutter, between types of occupation and special forms of deafness, between prescribed methods of speech therapy and successful restoration of speech to persons deprived of the power through injury or disease, between certain spatial arrangements and amount of learning. In the area of the normal,

---

16. A. Whitney Griswold, "This Tongue-Tied Democracy," *Vital Speeches* 21 (November 1, 1954), p. 829.

researchers are trying to determine whether women are more susceptible to certain forms of persuasion than are their male counterparts, whether presentations airing one side of an argument are more influential than those which offer two, whether certain personality traits are more closely correlated with effective group leadership than are certain others, whether definite relationships exist among sociopolitical conditions and the dominant speech theory of any given period, and so on. Thus, in many ways and in varied areas, professionals in the field of oral communication are exploring the endless problems associated with the process which enables *man to commune with man,* and more—which provides *the only true intimacy, the merger of soul with soul.*

This unique process is best characterized by a paradox which is implied in the previous statement, namely: "Man can communicate only what he has in common with other men, but that each communication is properly individual." While, as a highly complex process, it is rooted in the conventions of symbolization (with standard symbols *and* standard experiences), it is also shaped by the peculiarities of specific people, specific places, and definite times. While it is true that every normal member of a society draws from a common reservoir of symbols, experiences, and values, the application of them is determined by individual interpretation. Whether it be employed by the Swahili natives of Africa, the nomadic Eskimos of the frozen north or former presidents of the United States, whether it is applied in law courts, in Congress, in church, school or home, the process of speech inevitably includes individual idiosyncracies of *attitude, thought, bodily action, voice,* and *language.* And, according to how these are proportionally modified as they become more or less integrated with the others, the total act of speech (the total attempt at oral communication) will become either a success or a failure. (See Figure 1.)

Of all these factors which help to determine the nature of an individual act of oral communication, least appreciated are the *attitudes* of the persons involved. For purposes of this discussion, attitudes shall be conceived of as learned and relatively stable tendencies to respond in predetermined fashion to certain objects or situations. The attitudes held by each person develop out of his experiences and are shaped particularly by social interaction. With but a moment's reflection most of us can recall many personal attitudes that reflect time, place, and status of birth, early schooling, religious training, as well as other social experiences. With but a moment more, we realize these same attitudes were shaped during situations or experiences especially dominated by oral communication. No group of attitudes evidences a closer bond with the process of oral communication than those which each person forms about the "self." In like manner, few groups of attitudes demonstrate a more positive effect upon individual communicative prowess than those of self. Most psychologists and philosophers appear to agree with George Mead's observation that the self-concept is based upon the concepts others have manifested towards us which, in turn, help to determine our behavior patterns.[17] For example, a child knows that he is good or bad as a result of what he is told by parents, teachers, and friends; a young lady comes to know herself as pleasant, charming, and attractive when others react by telling her so; a business man considers himself successful, friendly, and capable because the verbal (and nonverbal) reactions of others have helped him shape such conclusions. And so it goes.

It is this same phenomenon which underlies the problem of stage fright. Largely due to earlier experiences in which one sees himself or others suffer from incompetence, certain exaggerated reaction patterns develop regarding oral communication situations. There arises an over-awareness of the self, an abnormal concern with the distintegrative processes and an inability to engage in effective communication. While it is true that most individuals advance from adolescence to old age with a lack of introspection, it does not necessarily follow that all persons are qualified to engage in such activity, nor that all persons will profit from it. There is much to be said for the view that "soul-searching" could encourage a distorted view of the searcher, the world and life generally.

Properly analyzed, the symptoms of stage fright—perspiring hands, "cotton mouth," trembling knees, and "butterfly" stomach—are seen to be but normal physiological reactions to an apparent threatening situation. Without such reactions, one would be either unconscious or dead. These are the same symptoms, essentially, which occur whenever one faces a situation which harbors real or imagined opportunities for punishment or failure: athletic contests, social events, intellectual competition, and the like. History records that famous speakers, whatever their proficiency, have always experienced such symptoms. The essential difference between the novice and the professional is that the latter channels the energy behind such symptoms into his talk, while the novice permits this same energy to impede his attempts. The efficient communicator recognizes these symptoms as normal and feels free to engage in bodily action which is appropriate and which acts as a release for his pent-up energy.

In each of the simplified instances just cited, the effects of such attitudes upon one's ability to communicate are obvious. The degree of emotional adjustment and mental objectivity is reflected in the organization of thoughts, choice of words, tone of voice, bodily actions, and the like. So it is with attitudes regarding others.

17. George Mead, *Mind, Self and Society* (Chicago: University of Chicago Press, 1934), pp. 135-36.

Beyond few obvious factors, to know that an individual is an American or a Frenchman or a German is not enough to enable anyone to say what his attitudes are towards specific situations or, more particularly, towards people. However, exposed to a series of speaking performances by this same individual, one would be able to make some valid judgments concerning these same attitudes. Basic *awareness, respect, sensitivity, flexibility,* and *understanding* tend to reveal themselves through one or all of the interrelated aspects of speech. Perhaps here more than anywhere else are revealed the important ethical standards which bind an individual to his society. Here, more than anywhere else, the individual defines his goals, ambitions, and responsibilities; here, in his attitudes towards others, either rests the driving force that could reduce civilization to the level of the ants, the lizards, and the snakes, or move it forward to greater gains and more impressive glories.

In truth it would appear that the perennial problems of civilization—Grecian difficulties epitomized by Demosthenes, Roman tribulations voiced by Cicero, medieval problems phrased by Dante, Renaissance confusions emphasized by Machiavelli and Galileo, and modern crises crystallized by Hitler, Stalin, or McCarthy—are not scientific or technological; rather they are ethical problems of persuasion; they are problems created by the attitudes of man towards man, and perpetrated by the unethical use of the basic process of communication: speech.[18] Is it not obvious that among other things one's attitudes toward others would dictate his selection, organization, and presentation of the facts of any given case? Is it not patent that proper attitudes towards others such as awareness, respect, sensitivity, flexibility, and understanding furnish the internal gyroscope which permits the process of speech to be used mainly for *communal* rather than *individual* gain? Is it not easily discerned, as shown in Figure 2, that anyone interested in improving his ability to communicate orally must be as intimately concerned with his attitudes as he is with his ability to articulate the symbols of the language?

A second major aspect of this important and complicated process of speech is *thought*. Whatever the precise relationship between *thought* and *speech*, certainly it is that good, effective speech includes all aspects of thought ranging from signal responses to reflective judgments. Various speaking forms from conversation through formal debate—if they are to be effective—must include the basic processes of joining, modifying, or diminishing the materials furnished to us by our senses. In terms of perceptions, for example, the speaker must be aware of the speaking situation

---

18. Richard McKeon, *Thought, Action and Passion* (Chicago: University of Chicago Press, 1954), p. 4ff. See also William H. White, Jr. *Individualism Old and New* (New York: Menton, Balch, 1930) pp. 87-88.

itself; he must manifest the ability to identify a *need* for communication (this is part of the difficulty outlined by Dr. Griswold in his claim that this is a tongue-tied democracy); he must also be able to discriminate among the various elements of the situation: the nature of the listener, the time, the place, the nature of the subject, and so on.

In addition to basic realizations, the speaker must be capable of certain interpretations. Among other things, he must have effective recall and the capacity to relate bits of knowledge; he must, in many instances, make instantaneous (and valid) inferences, exercise good judgment, and be capable of lucid, rewarding imagination. He must be accomplished in all these, and still more, for the ultimate end of these perceptions and interpretations is to order and arrange the raw material so that effective communication can be achieved.

This phase of ordering and arranging includes an *external* as well as an *internal* division. External ordering refers to the organization and/or adjustment of certain relations between speaker and listener (perhaps the listener is predisposed to reject whatever this speaker offers), between message and listener (perhaps the ideas are too difficult and demand greater elaboration for this particular audience), between message, time and place (perhaps the ideas are too controversial or too difficult to be presented completely at this time and in this place) and so forth. External ordering has to do with the organization of the phases of a communicative situation over and above the message itself; it has to do with the *plan of the whole.* Internal ordering concerns itself with the organization of the specific ideas which constitute the message. It is here that the speaker (either prior to the actual speaking event or during it) decides the precise sequence in which his ideas will be uttered; it is here that he determines the relative importance of his ideas, matters of cumulation and climax, points of elaboration, and the like. The phases of thought included in the process of speech, therefore, consist of discovering, noting, interpreting, and ordering bits of knowledge immediately applicable to any given speech situation. These phases will be analyzed more thoroughly at another point in this work.

A third major aspect of the speaking process is *bodily action.* This refers to the patterns of activity which most people think of when hearing the word *delivery* as applied to speech. As with Demosthenes, most people would cite this phase of the entire process as being the most important. Unlike Demosthenes, however, contemporary champions of delivery would be thinking solely of gesture and movement. Properly, bodily action in speech, that is, the physical action which forms a specific part of every speaking occasion, consists of three phases: (1) the sensory phase or the reception of stimuli from the surrounding environment (the operation of the senses of audition, vision, touch, kinesthesis); (2) the associative phase

Nature of Communication

or the integration of various neural activities which usually takes place in the cerebral cortex, but which may include such lower parts of the brain as the cerebellum; (3) the effective phase or the activity or completion phase which demands the action of muscles and glands. The most obvious aspect of this last phase is, as has already been mentioned, gesture or movement. And perhaps because of its obvious nature, it is this part which has blossomed forth to a point where it is easily confused with the whole. True, awkward and irrelevant movements have often served to confuse, indeed, to belie the meaning of oral symbols used by a speaker; however, it does not follow—as some of the older elocutionists would have us believe—that most effective communication will come with improvement in and emphasis on gesture. As a supplement to and the clarifying agent of other aspects of the total process, normal gestures characteristic of the individual furnish positive aid to all speakers. Equally important, though less frequently considered, is the role played by covert muscular activity like the neuromuscular activity related to breathing, posture, and movement.

Directly dependent upon bodily action is *voice*, the fourth major aspect of the total process of speech. Within the human species, voice is produced as a result of the integration of four major activities. The first of these is breathing, the process of respiration which provides the force for human voice. Unlike the respiration which helps to sustain life, breathing for speech includes inspiration and controlled expiration. The second of these major activities which produces voice is phonation, the oscillating action of the vocal folds resulting from the passage of the breath stream upon expiration. The third activity involved in human voice production is resonance, amplification, and reinforcement of sound waves in the cavities and occasionally in the solid structures of the upper body. After respiration, phonation, and resonance have produced a steady stream of sound, articulation, the fourth activity, produces the distinctive sounds characteristic of particular cultures. The tongue, lips, teeth, jaw, and palate act as modifying agents which shape the resonators and help form the various consonants and vowels peculiar to each language.

Through the ages—in one form or another—people have believed that *voice reveals personality*. "Let me hear his voice," they say, "and I will tell you what kind of man he is." While the statement is, of course, exaggerated, it is nevertheless true that people *do* use voice as an indicator of personality, and with some justification. The pitch, volume, quality, and rate of an individual's voice do vary during changes in temperament and, from the layman's point of view, certain vocal patterns are characteristic of certain temperaments. (Chapter 6 will deal with voice more extensively.)

In addition to attitude, thought, bodily action, and voice, the fifth and final process of speech is *language*. And this, it will be recalled, is where the discussion began with the matter of symbolization. As used in speech, symbolization means spoken sounds or combinations of sounds which form words. The individual speaker's symbolic prowess is partially revealed by his diction (choice of words) and his composition. Diction involves use of personal vocabularies; composition involves a regard for matters of grammar and style. Since habits of style change and since style should reflect an adjustment to the needs of the audience and the occasion, effective speakers continually work to develop a facility of varied styles. This, too, will be discussed more fully later.

SUMMARY

The previous thoughts have been focused on man's system of symbolization and the involvement of that system in both nonverbal and verbal communication. This ability of man to transform his experiences into ideas and in turn into symbols which he can manipulate with purpose and effectiveness is his sole liberating agent. The artificial bond between symbol and meaning, if not evaluated properly, leads him into confusions and misunderstandings which may be as tragic as they are comical. Effective communicators exercise care in defining a common meaning between themselves and their listener-readers. Moreover, the careful communicator realizes that he transmits his intended message in addition to several meta-messages which he may not intend.

Verbal communication, whether written or oral, is man's most common tool for social interaction. The most important of the two verbal modes, the oral, also proves to be the most complicated. It involves social traditions and experiences which are shaped and interpreted before they are offered as public utterances. When they are, it is as a result of the coordination of the speaker's attitudes, thoughts, bodily action, voice, and language.

PRACTICAL REMINDERS

Propositions

1. Man's thoughts are shaped by the nature of the language he uses in conceiving and expressing them.

2. Man draws from and contributes to society's reservoir of traditions every time he seeks to communicate.

3. Man communicates with man by verbal and nonverbal means and usually combines these in every communicative act.

4. Oral communication is a complex and dynamic tool useful in the development of both the individual and his society.

Exercises

1. With some friends, try to establish an extended communication for a period of fifteen minutes *without using* speech, writing, or formalized pantomime. At the conclusion of the period, compare reactions *before* messages are compared.

2. List as many occupations as possible which *do not* require a direct or indirect dependence upon oral communication for their creation, maintenance, or development.

Readings

BLACK, MAX, ed. *The Importance of Language.* Englewood Cliffs, N. J.: Prentice-Hall, Inc., 1962.

BOIS, J. J. *Explorations in Awareness.* New York: Harper & Row, 1957.

BOIS, J. J. *The Art of Awareness.* Dubuque, Iowa: Wm. C. Brown Company Publishers, 1966.

CASSIRER, ERNST. *Language and Myth.* New York: Harper and Bros., 1946.

GOLDSCHMIDT, WALTER R. *Exploring the Ways of Mankind.* New York: Holt, Rinehart, and Winston, 1960.

MASLOW, A. H. *Toward A Psychology of Being* (Revised). Princeton, N. J.: D. Van Nostrand, 1968.

MASLOW, A. H. "A Theory of Metamotivation: The Biological Rooting of the Value-Life," *Journal of Humanistic Psychology* I (1967): 93-127.

RAHSKOPF, HORACE G. *Basic Speech Improvement.* New York: Harper & Row, Publishers, 1965.

REIK, T. "The Psychological Meaning of Silence," *The Psychoanalytic Review,* 55 (Summer, 1968): 172-186.

TRAGER, G. L., and HALL, E. T. "Culture and Communication: A Model and an Analysis," *Explorations* 3 (1954): 137-149.

COMMUNICATION
(Sharing)
VERBAL

(Sharing is effected through the use of conventionalized symbols. Generally, confusions arising over the use of these symbols can be settled by recourse to a source which records the acceptable meanings associated with these symbols, i.e. dictionaries, printer's code books, Morse Code Manuals, Driver Manuals.)

        Oral   Visual
        Written   Aural

NONVERBAL (Tacit)

(Sharing is effected through the use of symbols, which, although not yet specifically codified by the society, are associated with broadly accepted meanings.)

Time
- Order
- Cycle
- Depth
- Rhythm

Space
- Physical
  - Personal
  - Public
- Abstract
  - Personal
  - Public

Form
- Macroform
  - Oral
    - Face-Face, Group, Radio, Television, Tapes, Phone

Form (Continued)
- Macroform
  - Visual
    - Pictures, Lights
    - Graphics, Color
  - Aural
    - Sounds, Music, Silence
  - Written
    - Memos, Letters, Print
- Microform
  - Monologue-Dialogue
  - Arguments
    - Inductive
    - Deductive
  - Silence

Action
- Posture
- Gesture
- Movement

FIGURE 1

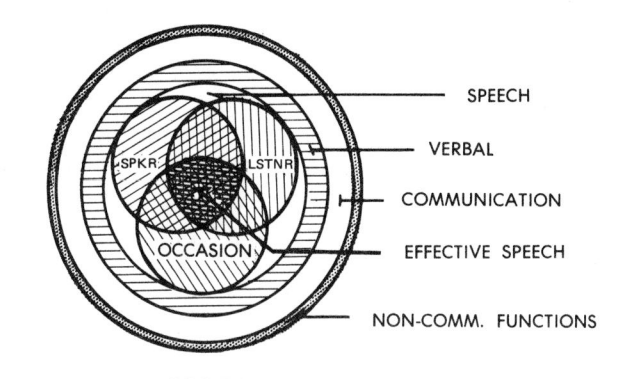

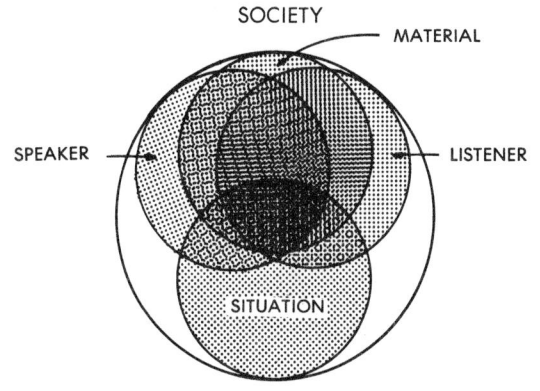

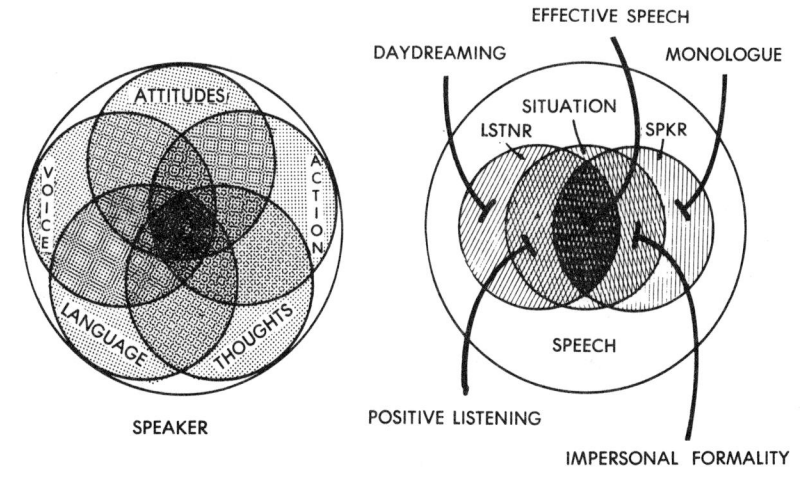

FIGURE 2

FIGURE 3

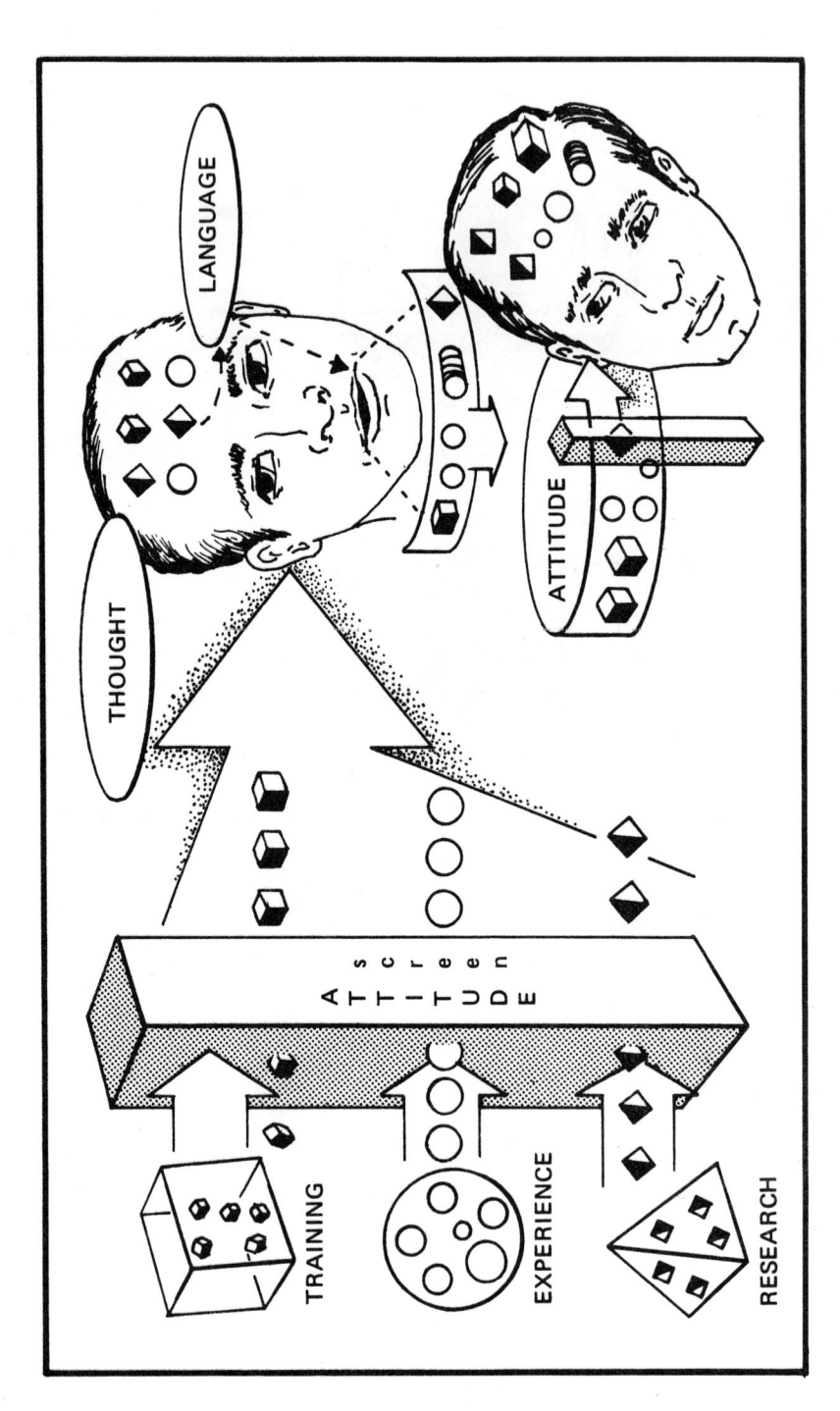

Chapter 2

PRINCIPLES OF EFFECTIVE ORAL COMMUNICATION

The task of the competent oral communicator is to understand the nature of communication so he may appreciate the reasons for any of the rules he seeks to apply in concrete situations.

Because it is dynamic and heavily dependent upon human activity, oral communication can never be analyzed or reproduced with such precision as to guarantee the amount of prediction and control experienced by those who work in the physical sciences. Nevertheless, as a result of improved understanding and better methodology, this fundamental human activity has been explored enough to permit the formulation of various basic principles which will enable man to get beyond his trial-and-error behavior. Today's world, filled with complexities of every sort, does not allow for the same sort of reasoning which helped man to escape from the jungle; "common sense" reasoning must give way to that which allows for a greater frequency of success. Principles must replace guesses and purposeful action must supplant trial and error activity, especially in an area as important to the overall health of society as is oral communication.

For over 2500 years in Western civilization, the discipline of speech communication has been marked by the careful metamorphosis of a set of principles which have taken on the flavor of specific times and special societies. Each modification has been an attempt toward better understanding and greater effectiveness; every alteration was proof of man's appreciation of the dynamic, viable, and fundamental nature of oral communication. Through the years, tested in the crucible of demanding societies, many specific rules have been preserved and transmitted from generation to generation. However, while the specific "how to" rules have been passed along, the broader principles explaining and supporting those rules have not been as regularly transmitted. In other words, the "how" has been more regularly passed on than the "why." When this occurs, rules turn into sterile dictators which help to produce automatons; things appear to get done and no one stops to question the rationale behind the action. In moments of apparent progress, there is no pressing need to know the *why* of an action which is working. However, faced with enough instances of failure or even continuous abrasion, the lack of knowledge concerning *why* can only guarantee the monkeylike trial-and-error behavior mentioned earlier. When someone knows the *why* of any activity (from typing to speaking), in the event that his list of *how's* proves inadequate, *he can shape new how's based upon his understanding of the reasons behind the how's.* Where the principles of oral communication have been studied and modified in conjunction with the rules, they have reflected the specific needs and values of the society which shaped them. In this way, by studying the principles of oral communication practiced and transmitted by a certain society, one can tell something of the nature of that society. Currently, for example, the strong democratic emphasis reflected in a large part of the Western world will show itself in the principles which guide the art of communication as employed by our contemporaries. Thus, the principles which follow represent an attempt to describe (and prescribe) effective communication within a society which is very largely democratic in environment.

PRINCIPLE A

In its effective state, oral communication is organized, meaningful, and selectively particular.

The principle observes the characteristic paradox mentioned in Chapter 1: Man can communicate only that which he shares in common with other men but each communication must be individual and particular. Despite its roots in social agreements and its characteristic of being a public phenomenon (even during the moments of conversations with oneself), oral communication is always individual, personal, and private. Both speaker and listener react by their own unique interpretations of the verbal aspects of speech. Whatever the nature of these interpretations, they always reflect the individual's desire for order and meaning. If what he hears and sees is not ordered and clear, the listener will either reject it or instill order and meaning to fit his personal needs. Thus, the sports-minded child, learning the Lord's Prayer without the benefit of society's meaning and with minimal knowledge of its language, might well recite: "Our Father who got in heaven, allowed the tie game." He might say *sparrow grass* for *asparagus* or *dandy lions* for *dandelions.* The immigrant from Mexico, hearing the Star-Spangled Banner for the first time, could easily repeat the first words as "Jose can you see;" or say *Lake Champagne* for *Lake Champlain.* The uneducated status-minded auditor can easily (and intentionally) be misled by speakers who, known for their opposition to education, ask: "Do you know that students are allowed to *matriculate* at Podunk University? That professors force students to show their *theses* before they are allowed to graduate? That male students are allowed to have *discourses* with females?"

Realizing this, the competent speaker makes certain that his entire communicative adventure is ordered, developed, and maintained in such fashion as to permit his meanings to fill the dominant needs of the listener. To do so, of course, the successful oral communicator maintains a constant appreciation for the role of the listener as an influential factor in prescribing the nature, scope, speed, and direction of speech efforts. And he finds this to be especially true when the listener interprets situations as confusing, ambiguous, threatening, or otherwise unpleasant.

In similar fashion, the sensitive speaker acknowledges the influence of this tendency to organize and inject meaning when, with the proper audience, time, and place, he shouts *ten-hut* instead of *attention;* answers a question with a long, fixed stare instead of words; overlooks the use of a wrong word in a question phrased by a foreigner; or pauses purposefully and responds to a heated and rapid challenge with slow, well-modulated, and carefully chosen words.

PRINCIPLE B

The dynamics of oral communication result from the psychophysical aspects of the immediate environment.

Unlike its written counterpart, oral communication can only be revealed in an "unfolding" process which is within the control of the individual speaker. No one can ascertain with certainty precisely what direction and color the speaker's thoughts will take until he releases them—and this includes the speaker himself, in many instances. This very act of unfolding contains within it the privilege and the *responsibility of modification, of adaptation to the changing needs of the speaker, listener, or occasion.* And it is this very flexibility which makes the speech adventure unique and wonderful. As the product of a crisis, a loss of equilibrium between the inner and the outer environments of the speaker-listener complex, it reflects the changes occurring within as well as *between* individuals. The degree of this imbalance varies with the factors involved in each specific situation; it may range from that created by the presence of another, who does not fully understand, to that created by one, who is definitely opposed. The attempt to adjust the balance, to reestablish what is termed homeostasis in medical psychology,[1] is the continuing goal of all speakers

1. G. K. Yacorzynski, *Medical Psychology* (New York: The Ronald Press Company, 1951), p. 23.

and the occasional achievement of some. This is precisely why the essence of good speech and good speakers is *flexibility*; this is precisely why such things as "canned" speeches (or speakers) are both a travesty and a farce;[2] this is precisely why "ghost-written" speeches cannot possibly be as effective as those conceived, delivered, and *modified in the process of delivery by the speaker*.

Toward this end, the competent communicator recognizes that, as a viable art form, good communication manifests a subtle balance between content and form. Because oral communication is not a science, there is no way of knowing the precise degree of emphasis to be exercised by either the content or the form. Only the mind of a sensitive and intelligent man can create the effective proportion which can contribute more than either offers singly. In any given situation, for example, the idea may well be eclipsed by the form—and for valid reasons. Someone seeking to overcome the charge of being a "shoddy thinker" may well highlight the form in order to achieve his goal. The parent attempting to demonstrate good thought to his child, the lawyer arguing a case before a superior court, the researcher presenting his results before a professional society, each might choose to structuralize his communication in this fashion. This is not to say such an imbalance, however slight, ought to be the standard. It is to say there are instances when the presence of form should be made more obvious in view of the final goal; that, conversely, there may be instances where the presence of other than a very loose and vague form would result in the annihilation or rejection of the idea.[3] In the final analysis, the sensitive speaker notes that the precise balance between form and idea is determined by the dynamics of the immediate situation, but in any case, good communication most generally reveals the strength of a real, albeit unobtrusive form. The absence of such an appreciation is readily evident in the actions of an overzealous and poorly educated debater who must always discuss in terms of stock issues, definitions, and phrases; in the speaking habits of the dedicated but misguided teacher who must always employ the Socratic method in his daily interactions; in the behavior of the well-intended executive whose communicative efforts always reflect the latest fad in human relations.

PRINCIPLE C

The proper concern of the oral communicator in any given act of communication is the satisfaction of his responsibility as a social organism.

2. Note the unbelievable news item in *The Wall Street Journal*, September 8, 1966, p. 1, which announces the availability of a teaching machine designed to produce "instant orators."
3. Saint Augustine, *On Christian Doctrine*, translated by D. W. Robertson, Jr. (New York: The Liberal Arts Press, 1958), p. 37.

Principles of Effective Oral Communication

Oral communication, as a communion among humans, is always a compromise between the intentions of the speaker and the expectations of the listener. But more than this, it is first an act of compromise between personal needs and social requirements. As has already been observed, this wonderful and dynamic activity serves both the individual and his society by acting as the tool for the development of both. At any one time, therefore, a conflict often exists over which of the two ends shall dominate during that venture; at other times, a constantly shifting role is assumed so that each goal is partially fulfilled. As a parent, for example, one usually strives to maintain the superiority of the social purpose in his communications with his children. However, as a human being with personal needs of his own, the parent occasionally engages in communication which is more an expression than a communion, more a release for pent-up frustrations than an exercise in guiding the concepts being developed by his offspring. And properly so, for no one can be perennially and exclusively concerned with his social obligations during every act of communication. Even if possible, it ought to be discouraged since it stifles the development of that individual and thereby reduces his value in future actions. In a word, the oral communicator's first responsibility as a social organism is the proper development of himself through the maintenance of a regular and fluid mobility between his internal and external environments.[4]

In terms of his personal needs, the sensitive speaker is aware of his need for constant contact with his two worlds (inner and outer) and his need to maintain a bridge between them. He notes, also, that his ability to speak helps him to locate and define his doubts, confusions, feelings, and moods for himself even before he is interested in conveying them to others. Is there anyone in contemporary society who has grown to maturity without the experience of speaking *with* and *to* himself?[5] Can there be those who, *in the process of describing a concept to others*, have never come to see it more clearly themselves? Every act of oral communication is a creative act in that it requires the speaker to reach into the general mass of thoughts or feelings which he stores inside of him (and to which he adds regularly), to identify one, give it the best shape possible from those available in the language he is using at the moment, and then try to color, stretch, smooth, scratch, and fluff it in such a way as to make it recognized and appreciated by a particular listener. In developing the formless into viable shapes, the individual changes his own storehouse of experiences and thus he changes himself, for it is bits of himself which are contained

---

4. See Carl R. Rogers, "Communication: Its Blocking and Its Facilitation." *Northwestern University Information* 20 (April 21, 1952), pp. 9-15.

5. Man has now discovered this process to be indispensable to the successful development and performance of complicated computers. See John Pfeiffer, "Machines That Man Can Talk With," *Fortune* (May, 1964), pp. 2-8.

in his every act of communication—from the breath expended to the thoughts conceived. In truth, the sensitive speaker can say:

> I am pressed between the cutting edges
> of my own teeth.
> Tossed by the movements of my tongue,
> Shaped by the action of my cheeks,
> Bathed in the sound of my own throat,
> Lost in the shadowy regions of my own mind.

For him, particularly, speech offers creation and distinction; it provides continuity to his individual nature and furnishes the means for transporting himself from the depths of introspection to the heights of social communion. It is, in the final analysis, the only true image of his naked, mercurial, and personal being.

In terms of his social responsibility, the conscientious speaker reveals his indebtedness to the society of which he is a part by careful, discrete and meaningful use of his power to affect the life of another. Just as speech proves important in his own continuing development, it proves necessary to the life and growth of the speaker's auditors. As shall be seen in Chapters 7 and 8, the oral communicator claims the right, however temporary, to shape and direct the life of another human being. As a parent, teacher, friend, or even a stranger, the speaker prescribes exactly how the next few moments of another person's life are to be spent. By asking a question, responding to one or purposely failing to do either, the speaker contributes or detracts from the maturation of the auditor. By clarifying alternatives, defining a universal mood, reinterpreting a half-truth or acting as a catalyst who "delivers in rain what he gathers as mist," the oral communicator contributes to the progress of his fellows. The contribution is made by a sensitive human who identifies the need in his fellow beings for sustenance of mind and spirit as well as body. Thus does the communicator champion the "I-Thou" philosophy.[6] He champions the thought that since speech is the revealer of psychological universes, the barometer of internal pressures and the mirror of the soul,[7] the necessary counterpart of the much-defended freedom of speech is the freedom of silence which he must permit his listener.

As a social organism sharing the privileges of society's heritage and exercising a responsibility of contributing to its progress, the serious student of oral communication maintains the moral obligations inherent in

---

6. Martin Buber, *Between Man and Man* (New York: The Macmillan Company, 1948), pp. 175ff.
7. Harry Overstreet, *The Mature Mind* (New York: W. W. Norton & Company, Inc., 1949), pp. 13-41.

all good discourse.[8] These include the obligation to make and act on competent value judgments regarding people and their ideas without engaging in false human relations or callous indifference; to know and act on the difference between a sincere respect for the worth of the individual and an indiscriminate approval of *any concepts* articulated by *any* speakers. In addition, the oral communicator has an obligation which, although less obvious and rarely discussed, is part of his responsibility to return something to society; it is the obligation to foster and preserve the image of speech as a viable and basic mode of human interaction. This is done best, of course, by using it to create an image and to discourage any use to the contrary. In a word, the good communicator exercises his responsibility for the preservation of *good* communication by employing *good* habits of speaking and listening *whenever* and *wherever* he communicates.

PRINCIPLE D

The qualities of communication are improved in proportion as the qualities of the communicator are improved.

If anything in the preceding chapters can be said to be a recurring theme, it is that the nature and importance of oral communication requires attention which must be deep and sustained if it is to be improved. One cannot improve it by acquiring a thin veneer of thumbnail jokes, increased vocabulary, and refined gestures any more than one can improve his health by dabbing himself with iodine or taking "pep" pills. Nor can it be improved by three-day institutes or two-week seminars. As with matters of health, oral communication requires development in the more basic areas of man's interior self: attitudes toward himself and the world, thought patterns enabling him to shape those attitudes, knowledge furnishing thought, and a language sensitively handled to insure the depth and color necessary for the understanding and acceptance of thought. Intellectual nourishment of this kind will show itself by sound growth from within in much the same fashion as that derived from the physical nourishment taken in by daily meals. The taller, wider and deeper a man is intellectually, the more proficient he is as a communicator.

SUMMARY

With some, speech is an adventure; with others, it is their history. With some, speech is a personal conclusion; with others, it becomes a universal

---

8. See David Riesman, "Value in Context," *The American Scholar*, (Winter 1952/53), p. 35.

truth. In all, it is a public ordering of private awareness for social interaction, and as a man improves his private capacities his public interaction will also improve.

PRACTICAL REMINDERS

Propositions

1. Effective oral communication can never be epitomized by one example which can apply to all people and all ages.
2. The ingredients of every instance of oral communication—speaker, listener, time, place, and subject—all play a part in determining the success of the experience.
3. Speakers more interested in self-expression than in self-improvement will rarely become effective.
4. Any standard approaches to effective speaking, from jokes to phrases, hinder the speaker's effectiveness.

Exercises

1. Try to conduct a communication with a friend by responding to his queries or statements with only appropriate proverbs or adages.
2. Again, with a group of friends, arrange for a few to engage in regular and irrelevant responses to whatever is being said by some of the group who have not been forewarned of this exercise. Record their reactions and note how long this is allowed to continue before it is broken off by questions concerning the "strange behavior."

Readings

BRUNER, J. "On Perceptual Readiness," *Psychological Review* 64 (1957), 123-152.
FRAZER, J. G. *The Golden Bough.* New York: The Macmillan Company, 1949.
GREENBERG, A. "Is Communications Research Really Worthwhile," *Journal of Marketing* (January, 1967), 48ff.
HOVLAND, C.; JANIS, I.; and KELLEY, H. *Communication and Persuasion.* New Haven: Yale University Press, 1953.
KRECH, DAVID and CRUTCHFIELD, RICHARD. *Theory and Problems of Social Psychology.* New York: McGraw-Hill Co., 1948.
MORRIS, CHARLES. *Signs, Language* and *Behavior.* Englewood Cliffs, N. J.: Prentice-Hall, Inc., 1946.
ROGERS, C. *On Becoming a Person.* Boston: Houghton Mifflin Company, 1961.

PART II

ORAL COMMUNICATION
Method and Meaning

*Meaning is born
of method*

James O. Sneddon, Photographer
University of Washington *Alumnus*, Spring 1966
Used by permission.

Chapter 3

SKILLS OF THE SPEAKER–
SPEAKER-LISTENER ANALYSIS

Among the numerous experts in the field of communication, there are various definitions of the term persuasion. Some argue there is an important and definite distinction between education and persuasion. The thought is that insofar as one deals with information, persuasion does not enter the scene. The major criterion in this point of view is *facts*. Thus, if the material tends to be factual, if the speaker tends to present the facts as they were discovered, the attempt at communication falls into the category of educational or informative communication.

Others believe that in proportion as a speaker selects materials to be given, organizes and develops them to the satisfaction of the audience, matters of persuasion operate.[1] In other words, whenever an individual has his choice limited or prescribed as a consequence of additional information, his decisions are being directed and therefore persuaded. This applies as much to instances in education as it does to occasions peculiar to law courts. In both areas, much is said about presenting only factual material so that the listener can judge for himself. Yet, the time allotted, the procedures followed, and the facts selected have already defined the limits of the listener's choice. Further examples are legion whether drawn from areas of business, industry, religion, or the various professions. Whenever one man seeks to gather, organize, and present materials to another man, matters of persuasion must play a part.

It is in this broader sense of persuasion that philosophers have long described the problems of civilization as being problems of persuasion. Wars are fought not because we lack technology, but because people have failed in their attempts at persuasion. Overpopulation, smoking, vice, carnage on the highways, delinquency, and divorce all remain problems as long as failure marks the various attempts to persuade people to alter their

---

1. See Harold C. Martin, *The Logic and Rhetoric of Exposition* (New York: Henry Holt & Company, Inc., 1958), pp. 76ff.

behavior. Men work in harmony with each other in matters of religion, education, industry, and health as a consequence of successful, persuasive communication. Lack of harmony in each of these areas is an accurate index of unsuccessful attempts at persuasion.

Since the time man first recognized the importance of systematizing his attempts to communicate with other men, he has identified certain elements as basic to the matter of persuasion. These he has identified as the speaker, the message, and the occasion, all of which are related so as to produce a desired response in a particular listener. In short, every single act of communication is a definite specialized attempt by a speaker to *persuade a definite specialized listener at a definite specialized time.* At this point, therefore, it seems appropriate to discuss the roles played by speaker and listener.

SPEAKER ANALYSIS

Regardless of the age of the individual, irrespective of his walk of life, he tends to be influenced by the very nature of other people with whom he deals. For most of their young lives, children place their hope and trust in those adults with whom they have frequent and close contact. These, of course, are their parents. As they grow older, the shift in confidence and trust occurs—sometimes completely, sometimes partially—from parents to teachers to friends. In any large social unit from institutions to governments, adults are inclined to believe certain people and to distrust others. *And it is this appeal which,* in the ill-defined areas of communication, *carries much more impact than the arguments themselves.* With but a moment's reflection, we recall from our own experiences that from some people we are inclined to accept the strongest chastisement and from others we are inclined to reject an equally strong compliment. The early Greeks sought to define this reaction in terms of the listener's *integrity, competence,* and *goodwill.*

Integrity

In Chapter 1 mention was made of the ethical standards which bind an individual to his society. On the basis of mutual values, speaker and listener can proceed in their symbolic communion by effecting agreements, making commitments, and generally directing the course of many lives. Where there are conflicts in these values, inevitable questions of ethics arise: "What ought to be done?" "What is morally right at this point?" "Do personal values supersede those of society?"

Such questions are difficult to answer regardless of when they are asked and by whom. They represent the perennial struggle of mankind to relate to that which is true and good and constant. In the area of symbolic interaction—oral communication—the questions are especially pertinent since the great bulk of man's relationships with his fellows are conceived, developed, and maintained in this fashion. Given the democratic atmosphere mentioned in Chapter 2, the good communicator maintains his personal *homeostasis* by effecting a balance between the two conflicting sets of values—whenever they arise. At times, the communicator might well decide to *withdraw from the sharing process since conditions* will not permit a true sharing without severe distortion of one or the other set of values. Not enough emphasis is placed upon the thought that the communicator ". . . is nearly always at liberty to give up persuading an audience when he cannot persuade it effectively except by the use of methods that are repugnant to him. *It should not be thought, where argument is concerned, that it is always honorable to succeed in persuasion, or even to have such an intention.*"[2] From the time of Aristotle, if not before, it has been believed that ethical decisions are a reflection of a man's *ethos*, especially his integrity.

If in the course of prior publicity, or during the presentation of the speech itself, the audience is inclined to question the sincerity or consistency of the speaker, his message will be rejected regardless of its value. On the other hand, as we have repeatedly experienced, a communicator conceived by his audience (whether one or three hundred) to be consistent within himself, sincere in his desire to share with others while retaining the right to be his own man will have his message accepted—many times—in spite of an inherent weakness contained within it. But it must be remembered that the greatest force in the creation of an image of integrity is the speech act itself. It is as though here, in the presence of the audience, the speaker bares his innermost self. If the image of this self is of one who has read widely, who speaks only of what he firmly believes, and who has respect for the most important values of his society, his integrity will be established with that particular audience. If, on the other hand, his image is revealed as one who speaks opportunistically, who is inclined to handle ideas and feelings with the obvious mark of a shallow man, his integrity will be questioned. Unfortunately, our social experience is such that we have already recognized categories of men whose integrity is challenged automatically. Surely in describing an individual, you have heard others say he is "just a salesman." The thought here, of course, is that salesmen are inclined to say anything and everything so long as they can achieve their desired end. While this may not be true, the image has been

---

2. C. Perelman and L. Olbrechts-Tyteca (trans. J. Wilkinson and P. Weaver), *The New Rhetoric: A Treatise on Argumentation* (Notre Dame: University of Notre Dame Press, 1969), p. 25.

strongly created in our society and it is the *image rather than the fact* that directs the action of most people most often. Obviously, the easiest way to create the image of integrity is to be a man of integrity. Every listener, from single witnesses to multitudes, would prefer to associate with men in whom the inner man and outer man are as one. Particularly in this complex period of civilization, people are continually disturbed and repelled by those who pretend to be one thing while they are another. The fatigue derived from trying to measure a man by his communication is forcing most people to accept the alternative of simple and complete rejection of those who pose a problem. In special moments of crises, in times when actions as well as ideas appear to be so transient and viable persuasion assumes greater potency. The following principle, passed on to us from ancient civilization, has not lost its truthfulness through the passage of time: *The good speaker is the good man speaking well.* When such a speaker is figuratively dissected, one will find him to have a characteristic union of integrity and competence.

Competence

Rare is the situation where listeners will be persuaded by speakers who show an obvious lack of competence in the material being discussed. Obviously, a lay opinion about the treatment of a certain disease will not carry as much force as the opinion of a qualified medical doctor on the same subject. A talk by a member of the accounting staff arguing for test drillings in a certain area will be less effective than the same talk delivered by a geologist. Such obvious and complete qualification, however, is not always available or possible. The fluid nature of today's society demands that each person assume a variety of roles in the course of daily living. And for each role, however long it endures, we are expected to demonstrate a minimal degree of competence. As a father, husband, friend, schoolboard member, churchgoer, student leader, we are often expected to demonstrate our speaking competence whenever we speak. What value do we place on the comments of a childless father talking about child rearing? Of a bachelor speaking about the ideal marriage? Of a teen-ager about the trials and tribulations of the depression of the early 1930s?

Competence is gained through the wise and regular use of three major avenues of knowledge: *experience, training,* and *research.*

Today a popular notion is that experience is the best teacher. This false notion, more often repeated than understood, has led many persons to assume a negative attitude toward training and research. As a consequence, their own efficiency is quite well described by the nature of their past lives. Experience, in fact, is the worst teacher since it gives the test first and the lesson later. Learn by experience, for example, that iodine is poisonous to humans; that one should not stand in front of a turbojet engine when it is turned on; that wet fingers stuck into an electric socket could be fatal. Worse yet, experience is a poor teacher since it offers no controls to guarantee the learning of good habits instead of bad. For this reason, all experience is not necessarily good experience. One may learn by experience to become very good at being very bad.

Training is more efficient since material is learned in shorter time and in better fashion. One may, for example, move from the status of an amateur to civil engineer in approximately four to five years of intensive and directed training. To be sure, a better possibility would be to have a combination of training and experience. Even so, one can become quite rigid in his thinking and stereotyped in his habits if he restricts his endeavors to those learned by training and experience. Unless these two aspects are continuously broadened by regular research (reading, discussions, interviews) they will soon be outdated.

Continuous research is demanded in this age as man finds himself more and more removed from direct experience with his environment and no longer in direct, systematic, and sustained contact with the world of nature. As an intelligent citizen he finds it practically impossible to function without a dependence on certain mediators. Even with all of the advantages of jet travel and adequate finances, the average person can hardly travel through all of China, interview the heads of state in Europe, watch the Olympics in Rome, or become involved enough in the politics of emerging nations. Nevertheless, he is often required to act—symbolically or in reality—on the basis of information concerning events, places, and things, such as those mentioned above, which he has never personally experienced. In truth, the modern citizen's judgments and actions are governed largely by the nature and the efficacy of mediators which stand between him and the various phenomena making up his environment. Throughout the history of mankind certain individuals or groups have seized upon this opportunity and have sought to control others by directing the mediating agents.[3] Thus, the influence of man's nonpersonal sources (books, newspapers, radio, TV, other people, etc.) is profound enough to merit the attention of anyone interested in improving himself and his society.

Without question, the most extensively used source of information available to the literate man of the twentieth century is the printed word. So vast is this storehouse of information that no single system of classifying and recording available data exists. Nonetheless, certain more reliable systems have been construed in the attempt to reduce the complexity of the situation facing the average individual.

3. Overstreet, *op. cit.*, p. 227.

To begin with, the interested student of effective oral communication should become familiar with available libraries within his community. This should include, of course, those libraries located in the city, in newspaper plants, in colleges and universities, in smaller public and private schools, and in certain federal facilities such as army bases and so forth. Within each library, the student should note the location and special features of the reference rooms, periodical collections, card catalogues, and other particulars.

Reference rooms in most libraries contain such general source materials as dictionaries, encyclopedias (general and special), biographies, government records and so forth. In addition, most of them contain the major indices needed to locate information on specific topics. Among the more common indices of this sort, one should become familiar with *Poole's Index to Periodical Literature* (which records articles published in popular journals before 1900); *Readers' Guide to Periodical Literature* (which records articles published in popular journals after 1900); *International Index to Periodicals* (which records scholarly articles for the professional journals published since early 1900); *The New York Times Index* (which catalogues information published in *The New York Times* newspaper since its first publication); *Cumulative Book Index* (which notes the newest books issued each year). There are, in addition, the more specialized indices dealing with particular fields (*Index to Legal Periodical Literature, Education Index, Industrial Arts Index, Index Medicus*) or with particular journals.

After a good exploration of the reference rooms in the nearest libraries, the conscientious citizen should make himself familiar with the periodical collections available to him. During this investigation, he should try to determine the nature, extent, and location of the holdings. Many libraries keep two or three of the current issues of a periodical on open shelves and the back issues beneath these same shelves or in some stacks located nearby. In any event, the individual should be aware of the several categories of periodicals. From scholarly and accurate publications such as *American Scholar, Classical Review, Journal of the History of Ideas, Economist, Harper's Scientific American, Vital Speeches,* and others of this type, one can move to those more popular, less accurate publications which are available on corner newsstands. In making the decision of which periodical to use, one should consider that quarterlies are generally more concerned with accuracy of fact and depth of value than are weeklies, but no periodical is beyond the possibility of having serious error and prejudice. Finally, many libraries classify their newspapers with journals and will probably store them in the same area. Because most newspapers are under serious and continuing pressures to meet the competition, they tend to be less concerned with accuracy than with saleable news. Reporters, copy writers and copy readers and city editors usually work under pressures of speed and drama rather than calm reflection and prolonged investigation. Although some are more reliable, more consistent and less dramatic, the very nature of the industry argues against the probability that newspapers will ever become a major source of trustworthy information. Still, such papers as *The New York Times, The Christian Science Monitor, Washington Post,* and *The Wall Street Journal* have achieved reputations as competent chroniclers of daily events.

Card Catalogues, of course, list the books (and in some places, bound periodicals, pamphlets, etc.) available in any single library. Usually, books are catalogued alphabetically according to author, title and subject, and by virtue of a numbering system are located for the reader. Thus, if he wished a book by Egbert Erudite entitled *The Many Moods of Mount Rainier,* the researcher could look under *Erudite* or *Many Moods of Mount Rainier* or *Mountains.* In each place, he would find a card carrying essentially the same information, including a number in the upper left-hand corner telling him where the book is stored.

Knowing where to look for information is only the first part of the communicator's task, however. How he uses the source and what value he places on what he uses is the real test of an educated man. It is important, for example, to use an Encyclopedia only to obtain a broad view of the subject, gather insights into its relation to other subjects, and secure additional source citations. Periodical and newspaper information should be used to gather more details and interpretations, while specialized books and essays should be used to provide deeper and more reflective treatments. And the information gathered, regardless of the sources employed, should be recorded accurately on note cards.

All serious professionals, whether in business or education, rely heavily on the card system to record important information. Cards unlike notebook paper can be conveniently shuffled and reshuffled to suit changing patterns; cards can be used for single ideas or categories while notebook paper is not so conveniently employed. If each card were titled with temporary subcategories, preliminary information can be gathered and stored with less random activity. Moreover, if each card were coded by letter or number to match a system detailed on a master card, one would be spared the labor of recording the entire source name on each card. Thus, one card would be set aside as a major bibliographical card on which the full title, author, place, and date of publication were recorded. Opposite each source listed, the research could be a number or a letter. Thereafter, each card carrying information drawn from any of the sources shown on the master card would bear the number or letter assigned that source. With this system, the researcher is required to note only the specific page number in addition to the idea itself. Finally, all information should be recorded verbatim and set off by quotation marks to remind the researcher that paraphrases, if used, should be constructed only in the stage before organization of the outline.

Goodwill

Supported by integrity and strengthened by competence, the ability to communicate effectively is made applicable by the important quality of goodwill. It affects the communicative act in two ways: influencing the disposition of the listener and modifying the speaker's management of tools. From the time of the first philosophical truth, it has been recorded that humans appear predisposed to return kindness with kindness, compassion with compassion, charity with charity. The speaker who, through the selection and treatment of his topic and the nature of his style and the management of the occasion, inspires his listener's goodwill has already progressed more than halfway toward his goal. This is the quality which neutralizes malice, compromises hate, removes indifference, and motivates acceptance.

A speaker armed with insult and outrage and reflecting an insolent, overbearing, supercilious, reproachful, or indifferent attitude will be rejected outright. On the other hand, a speaker who demonstrates a knowledge of his audience and, because of it, a concern for their welfare and a respect for their capabilities will tend to be accepted by that audience.

Supported by integrity, strengthened by competence, and made applicable by goodwill, the ability to communicate becomes a power no other can give.

AUDIENCE ANALYSIS

The ultimate purpose of all communication is *audience response.* The very term audience is drawn from the presence of auditors; it refers particularly to a congregation of humans who came to hear the spoken word.

Despite a tradition of concern for uncovering the mysteries that control the behavior of the earwitnesses around him, the average person preparing to make a presentation will think more about himself than about his listeners. The problems that occupy most of his time will be those associated with his nervousness, the importance of the task, selection and preparation of audiovisual aids, and the like.

Yet, with proper reflection, even the most elementary speaker will realize that the solution to each of these problems varies with each audience. Sportsmen diagnose and act according to the strengths and weaknesses of a specific opponent while attempting to apply the principles of their sport; medical doctors prescribe for specific patients though they apply general principles of medicine; psychiatrists spend much, if not most, of their time analyzing the peculiar difficulties of the individual client before drawing from their training and experience to determine how certain therapy will be applied. So, as noted in Figure 3, when man seeks to communicate he must always do so according to the peculiar attitudes, desires, goals, and abilities of his specific "circle of witnesses" if he is to achieve his purpose.

Good audience analysis is the product of careful, systematic thought applied *before* and *during* the presentation. Easily the more extensive of the two, the analysis carried on before the presentation reflects much collecting and ordering of data from various sources for the purpose of selecting, arranging, and developing the presentation. On the other hand, the analysis carried on during the presentation reflects dynamic thought applied to data drawn from immediate audience response for the purpose of modifying or rearranging the presentation. In each instance, the analysis must make use of proper sources and specific kinds of information.

Audience Analysis Before the Presentation

Prior to the presentation, as much information as possible should be obtained to enable the speaker to prepare efficiently. Such information is best secured from sources beyond those noted in the earlier portion of this chapter. These include information from previous speakers, from associates of the proposed auditors, from meetings, from official records, and from popular as well as specialized publications which may carry details and general observations about individual auditors or the group to which they belong.

Perhaps the most awkward source of relevant information about the listener is the *questionnaire*, with the listener consciously supplying biographical material about himself. To be effective, questionnaires should be brief, simple, and discreet. If possible, personal contact explaining the nature of request should precede the administration of the questionnaire. And, finally, a greater percentage of return can be assured by providing the audience with a common time and place for the completion of the questionnaire. The average person finds it easier and less embarrassing to make out a questionnaire about his personal history if he is but one of forty people doing the same thing at the same time.

To this point, the discussion has been concerned with suggested sources of audience information which the speaker should avail himself of before preparing the presentation. Now, attention should be given to the *kinds* of information which should be obtained.

As mentioned earlier, regardless of the kind of information secured, a special attempt should be made to segregate fact from opinion. Too often otherwise-discerning speakers have expended needless time, money, and effort preparing a presentation based on ill-founded opinions of the audience. This is not to say that opinion is of no value; carefully gathered and clearly labeled opinion can, over a period time, achieve a consensus which is as important as fact. This is to say that, unless clearly marked, isolated opinion may be mistakenly used as fact to guide the preparation of a program.

Speakers can do a more efficient job of organizing programs and presentations if they know the *purpose* for which the audience is gathered. This purpose, whenever possible, should be phrased by the audience or an agency responsible for it. Again, needless error can be avoided by working with fact rather than assumptions. Occasionally, the speaker assumes that an audience is gathered for a particular purpose and organizes his material accordingly, only to find—and to his dismay—that he is in error and the presentation has failed because of it.

Knowledge concerning the *size* of the audience will often determine certain aspects of selection, organization, development, and delivery of the message. When speaking to a small, intimate group the speaker might profitably include more details than when speaking to large, unstable audiences. Applying this thought to matters of development, one can easily note that certain audiovisual aids are best suited to large audiences while others should never be used with audiences over fifteen or twenty.

If adaptation of the material to the audience is to be successful, it is imperative that the speaker know the needs, interests, and experiences of his listeners. In the absence of specific information about these factors, the speaker can do a good job of deducing this knowledge from the *age range* of the audience. Intelligent men have been doing just that for well over two thousand years. Aristotle, writing almost three hundred and fifty years before Christ, recorded the major characteristics of men in their youth, in the prime of their life, and in old age. He admonished the careful speaker to remember the differences in interest and experiences and plan his message accordingly.[4] Modern speakers would do well to heed the same admonition.

Though seemingly a minor matter, the careful speaker nevertheless considers the possible barriers to success created by the poor *physical condition* of his audients. It can be assumed, of course, that most persons are normal. However, such an assumption should not lead one to the point of excluding every other possibility. Very frequently, in order to insure the

---

4. Lane Cooper, *The Rhetoric of Aristotle* (New York: D. Appleton-Century Co., 1932), pp. xx-xxi.

success of a communication, special seating arrangements should be made to preserve the dignity of listeners, especially those who have special problems of hearing or seeing. A well-organized, well-prepared communication is worthless unless it can be seen and heard by those for whom it is intended.

As with physical matters, it can be assumed that the majority of audiences are composed of persons who enjoy a normal *psychological* state. Nevertheless, every normal individual has his special hopes, desires, and prejudices and unless the speaker is conversant with those held by his listeners, he may unwittingly offend and antagonize; equally significant, he will lose the advantages of locating the "doors to the audience's mind." Among other things, the speaker should strive to determine the listener's attitudes (pro or con) toward the company or organization represented by him; the program, project, or idea he discusses; his personality and the audiovisual aids he uses.

The listener's concept of *status* or his perception of his role in any given situation is also important knowledge for the speaker to gather. Properly defined, it will enable the speaker to select appropriate examples, language, tone, and general demeanor.

In addition, the careful speaker considers the *previous activities* of his potential listener. Will his previous activities render the audient restless, bored, hostile, or indifferent? Has he been listening to four or five presentations prior to yours? Will he listen to three more after yours? Has he just eaten? Obviously, the answers to these and similar questions may very well direct the course of preparation for the talk.

Finally, the speaker should attempt to discover the listener's prejudices toward general matters of living such as politics, religion, and recreational interests.

Also of importance is the knowledge of the listener's *capabilities*. More than years in school, this category should reveal the nature and scope of an individual's thought patterns. Is he habitually mesmerized by detail? Would he be at home with generalization and abstraction? Is much background or preparatory material needed to facilitate understanding and/or acceptance? Has the listener's past prepared him as an effective participant in situations of the sort being planned? Naturally, knowing something of the listener's training and experience will help the speaker secure answers to such important questions and thus avoid needless barriers in his quest for successful communication.

So much, then, for a discussion of the sources and kinds of information about the audience which speakers should seek before the presentation. The remaining part of this chapter will be devoted to the sources and kinds of information about the audience which the speaker should seek during the more formal communicative experiences.

Audience Analysis During the Presentation

A very important part of every efficient, dynamic operation—whether by machine or by man—is the control exercised by a feedback system. By carrying on a continuous evaluation of what *is* being done as compared with what *ought* to be done, the efficient organism or machine directs itself toward its ultimate task with a minimal amount of wasted effort. Unless he reacted to the hundreds of sensory stimuli sent into his brain to help direct his course of action, the average man would be of little value to himself or to the society to which he belonged as a civilized or social being. And yet, such persons do exist—some of them take the form of parents, teachers, researchers, and salesmen. The one characteristic they share is that they "put out according to plan regardless of immediate conditions." The effective parent, teacher, researcher, and salesman "puts out according to plan *unless* immediate conditions dictate otherwise." In a word, the effective communicator recognizes, appreciates, and uses feedback, which is the main tool of audience analysis *during* the communication; he is flexible!

The most important source of information regarding audience reaction to a communication is, of course, the audience itself. Whatever the mode of audience reaction, the speaker should be aware of the fact that his *eyes* and *ears* furnish him with most of the information to be gathered in such situations.

Doubtless the eyes play an important role in helping the speaker estimate the degree of his success or failure. By watching his audience carefully, the speaker can determine what portion of his message should be expanded or deleted, what aspect of his delivery needs to be modified, what listeners are or will be obstacles, and so forth. Conversely, the nature and scope of a speaker's eye contact very often serve to inform the audience about his degree of sincerity, competence, and goodwill. Most listeners feel uneasy in the presence of a speaker who continually averts his eyes; others are inclined to reject him and his proposal. The efficient speaker realizes that information gained through visual contact is as essential to a good presentation as the examples he uses to demonstrate his points.

This is also true of hearing. The speaker must be acutely aware of sounds emanating from the audience which are other than speech sounds. Restlessness, side conversations, excessive coughing, and applause are clues which the good communicator uses to guide his adjustment of material and delivery. Moreover, the sense of hearing furnishes the speaker with an obvious opportunity to monitor what he is saying. Too often presentations are rendered impotent by virtue of an unedited remark offered by a speaker who was not listening to himself.

Skills of the Speaker: Speaker-Listener Analysis

In addition to the main sources of information already cited which enable the speaker to analyze the audience during his communication, there are subliminal cues or impressions from sensory stimuli. These are things one feels about audience attitude without knowing why.

Of the kinds of information mentioned previously under the section dealing with audience analysis before the presentation, size and age-range estimates could most obviously be altered as a result of an on-the-spot analysis. Less obvious is the fact that other categories can be modified in this way.

Keen observation by a sensitive speaker can also confirm or deny previous estimates of the physical state of the listener. Most eye glasses and hearing aids can be seen equally well by trained or untrained speakers, but only the trained, sensitive speaker can detect the habitual, prolonged squint or the unnatural tilt of the head as symptoms of impaired vision and audition. It is also true that the competent communicator will recognize and use cues in the form of exaggerated posture, facial expressions, and incongruous behavior patterns (excessive doodling, whispering, dozing) to adapt his presentation to the immediate condition of his listener.

Less susceptible to on-the-spot analysis is audience prejudice regarding politics, religion, and hobbies. For information about such interests, the speaker must rely mainly upon the analysis made "by the smell of the lamp" prior to the presentation. As regards audience attitude toward such things as the occasion, the program, the concept, or the speaker, some aid is effected through on-the-spot analysis. In fact, it is conceivable that the immediate analysis would be of much more value than the prior analysis for determining such things as audience attitude toward the company, the speaker, the project, visual aids, and the like. At times, also, the speaker may note that the audience wishes to remain on a formal or informal basis. The speaker may aid his cause by adjusting to the mood established by the audience. One method of doing so is to use the name or title of various listeners in the presentation (with discretion) and/or during any question-and-answer period.

The speaker must continually evaluate cues to find answers to such questions as: Is he listening? Is he bored? Has he understood? Is he convinced? The only valid answers for such questions are drawn largely from the immediate response of the listener.

SUMMARY

The skilled speaker recognizes the need for analyzing his own strengths and weaknesses regarding his ability as a persuader. Toward this end, he strives to define and maintain his integrity as related to each communicative experience. Moreover, he analyzes and maintains a high level of competence on each occasion by making wise use of relevant experience, training, and research which strengthen his goodwill.

Since the ultimate purpose of all communication is audience response, competent speakers should make every effort to engage in an analysis of their audiences. This necessary analysis is actually twofold: (1) that engaged in prior to the presentation; (2) that engaged in during the presentation. Both require a knowledge of definite sources and kinds of information desired. Sources for prior analysis include permanent audience files, previous speakers, associates of listeners, formal meetings, personnel records, official publications, general publications, and questionnaires. Sources for analyses conducted during the presentation include eyes, ears, and subliminal cues. Kinds of information sought include audience purpose, size, names, age range, physical condition, psychological condition, and capabilities. (See Figure 3.)

PRACTICAL REMINDERS

Propositions
Speaker
1. A good speaker maintains a continuous evaluation of his source materials in the areas of training, experience, and research.
2. A good speaker maintains a healthy skepticism of all conclusions drawn by himself and his sources.
3. A good speaker maintains an "illusion of the first time" whenever he seeks to engage in serious communication with his family and friends.
4. Speakers who generate a feeling of respect and sincere concern for the audience are generally more successful than those who manifest indifference.

Audience
1. The single most important phase of communication is audience analysis.
2. Although susceptible to valid generalization about people, each audience has its own special psychology and *must be analyzed separately.*
3. Intelligent, critical audients are more readily persuaded by presentations which expose various sides of a problem as well as recommended solution.
4. Intelligent, critical audients must be given opportunity and time to draw occasional inferences.
5. With small audiences particularly, explicit adaptation by each speaker (to individual listeners, preceding speakers, immediate psycho-

physical conditions) tends to promote more rapid and lasting favorable impressions.

6. Listeners already favorably disposed toward the speaker, message, or program should be spread through the audience rather than seated in a group.

7. Attention and interest of listeners manifest themselves in waves rather than at some particular time during the presentation; *they must therefore, be considered throughout the presentation.*

Exercises
1. What attitude is revealed by the speaker in the following instances:
    a. "The bottle is half full." vs. "The bottle is half empty."
    b. "I have paid $20,000 on a $40,000 home." vs. "I owe $20,000 on a $40,000 home."
    c. "Why were those left out?" vs. "Why were those included?"
    d. "Speech is self-expression." vs. "Speech is social interaction."
    e. "I have an hour to rest." vs. "I must get up in one hour."
2. Speaker Research (see page 65).
3. After a talk has been prepared and outlined to be delivered to one audience, note what specific changes in language, examples or order would have to be made if the same subject were presented to a group of middle-aged women, an audience composed of career men in the Armed Forces, or a group of high school seniors.
4. Revise Lincoln's Gettysburg Address so that it can be delivered to a community of blacks and whites in a large American metropolis.
5. What possible effective adjustments might a good speaker make when, in the middle of his talk, approximately one-fourth of the audience leaves? When fifty or sixty persons are ushered into the room and proceed to fill up various empty seats throughout the room?

READINGS

ANDERSEN, MARTIN P.; LEWIS, WESLEY; and MURRAY, JAMES. *The Speaker and His Audience.* New York: Harper & Row, Publishers, 1964.

HOLLINGSWORTH, H. L. *The Psychology of the Audience.* New York: American Book Company, 1935.

HOVLAND, CARL J.; JANIS, IRVING L.; and KELLEY, H. *Communication and Persuasion.* New Haven: Yale University Press, 1953.

HOVLAND, CARL J. *Personality and Persuasibility.* New Haven, Conn.: Yale University Press, 1959.

KRECH, DAVID; CRUTCHFIELD, RICHARD S.; and BALLACHEY, EGERTON L. *Individual in Society.* New York: McGraw-Hill Book Company, 1962.

MARTIN, HAROLD C. *The Logic and Rhetoric of Exposition.* New York: Henry Holt & Company, Inc., 1958.

McCroskey, James C., and Mehrtey, R. Samuel. "The Effects of Disorganization and Nonfluency on Attitude Change and Source Credibility," *Speech Monographs* 36 (March, 1969), 13-21.

Rosnow, Ralph L., and Robinson, Edward J. *Experiments in Persuasion*. New York: Academic Press, 1967.

Sherif, Carolyn; Sherif, Musafer; and Nebergall, Roger E. *Attitude and Communication*. New York: Random House, 1967.

Tagiuri, Renato, and Petrullo, Luigi. *Person Perception and Interpersonal Behavior*. Stanford: Stanford University Press, 1958.

Speaker Research

Name:
Section:
Date:

Topic	Answers			Conclusion
	Source #1	Source #2	Source #3	
1. How many persons in the world speak the following languages? Italian Swedish Swahili Russian				
2. How many British soldiers were involved in the battle of Lexington and Concord? How many Americans?				
3. How many troops did the United States have in Vietnam from January to December, 1965? How many North Vietnamese troops were involved in that period?				

FIGURE 4

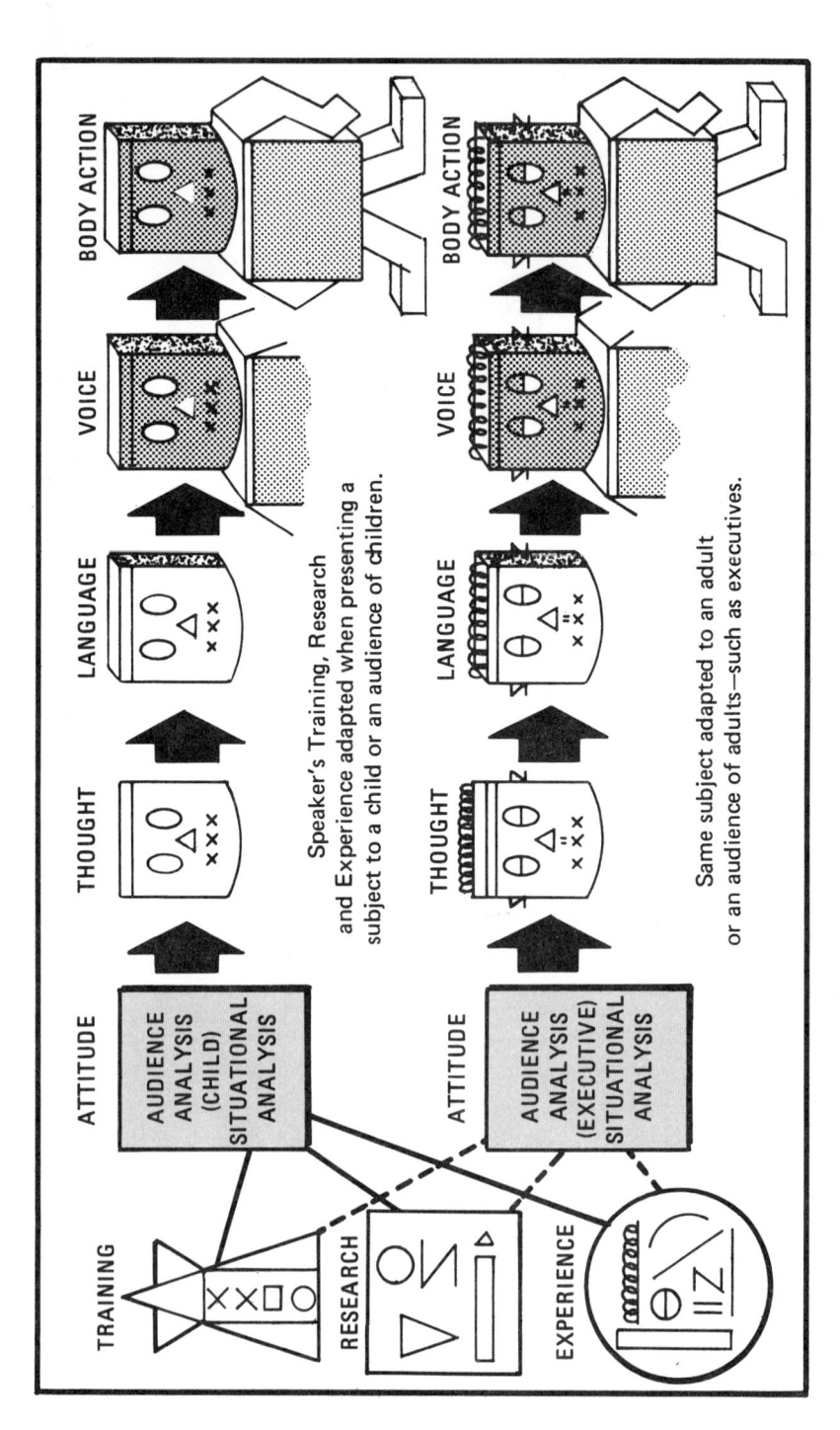

Speaker's Training, Research and Experience adapted when presenting a subject to a child or an audience of children.

Same subject adapted to an adult or an audience of adults—such as executives.

Chapter 4

SKILLS OF THE SPEAKER— MESSAGE ANALYSIS

Having considered the analysis of speaker-listener roles in the communicative experience, attention is now directed toward the third important ingredient: the message itself.

Principle A notes that effective speech is organized, meaningful, and selectively particular. As a corollary to this, it might be said that effective speech is purposeful speech. Throughout the years, scholars from Plato to John Quincy Adams have attempted to classify the various speech purposes and have generally agreed upon three: entertainment, information, and persuasion. As has already been observed, this test assumes it is more advantageous to treat all oral communication as having persuasion as its goal. The more subtle nuances which identify certain speaking experiences as entertaining but not informative and others as informative but not persuasive should be left for more advanced study. With this in mind, the following discussion emphasizes clarity, development, and style as significant factors in the probative force of any oral message.

CLARITY

Every act of communication can be placed upon a continuum of clarity from the one extreme represented by a column of numbers with a stated sum to that of a child defining love. Oral communication has at times the dual function of clarifying the speaker's ideas for both speaker and listener. Many times true understanding is acquired by the speaker only after his attempt to communicate with others. Primarily, however, the speaker's task is to make clear the ideas, moods, and attitudes he wishes to share with his fellows. The substance of the speaker's conversation should mean to the listener what it means to the speaker. In this period of great confusion, of thousands of distractions all calling for the average person's attention, of much sound and less sense, a speaker who wishes attention must express himself clearly enough to be understood at once. Few listeners have the time, inclination, or ability to sort through a jumble of words or unravel hopelessly tangled thoughts. Clarity in the meaning of a speaker's message may be affected by the nature of the subject and by its order of presentation.

Theme

An effective speaker must have some specific point to which all his comments are directed. Every act is thus founded on a central idea, feeling, mood, and so forth. It is the intellectual equivalent of deciding which target to shoot for in directing one's efforts during a hunt. Physically, economically, and psychologically it would be a waste to attempt to focus on two targets at the same time. While it may appear obvious and trivial, in everyday communication nothing is more common than to see this point ignored or forgotten. Conversations drip with four or five different topics jumbled together like so many pieces of laundry in an automatic washer. Their only relationship is that they are contained within the same receptacle in the same period of time—and perhaps they are soiled to the same degree.

Our laws demonstrate the need for curtailing this confusion by requiring courts and legislative bodies to specify in separate fashion each issue to be discussed. Parliamentary procedure allows for this clear definition of issues and provides the means whereby a clear sequence of topics and related discussions may be allowed. Yet, in most daily discussion, nothing provides for this needed precision except the sensitive habits of either speaker or listener. For example, a speaker may be endeavoring to discuss, formally or informally, the merits of land condemnation of offshore drilling procedures, but the listener has shifted to condemnation of private industrial corporations. It would be an unwise use of time and energy to continue the discussion unless the speaker firmly restricts the discussion to one theme or the other. Again, a speaker may be telling a chamber of commerce group that Standard Oil of California is dedicated to the goals of service, research, and economy but the greatest of these is service. The major portion of the discussion must focus on the assertion that service is the most important goal; the speaker should not get sidetracked into developing the important qualities of research and economy. These should be discussed only as their relative merits demonstrate the greater importance of service.

Incidental themes, arising naturally out of the discussion, often become so entangled with the main thought that they cloud it. And yet, just as often, these issues are not essential to the main idea. Definition is probably the best example of a minor issue which could easily mislead the speaker and confuse the listener. In attending to the merits of private enterprise versus public ownership, many speakers become bogged down in the definition of terms. The goal is to persuade the listener on the merits of private enterprise, not to school him on the intricacies of subtle legal definitions. It is enough to let him know what most people mean by the term and to let him know that the term will be used in this way. Most of the time and energy should then be directed toward supporting the declared issue.

Many speakers have failed to achieve their desired end simply because of the listener's inability to determine the exact nature of the topic being discussed.

Order

Structure, in the human society, is part and parcel of most experience available to the normal individual. From the architecture of cities to the architecture of feelings and thoughts, the average person is predisposed toward the acceptance of form and the rejection of the formless. As noted earlier, man as an organizing animal reacts to material presented in disorganized fashion by rejecting it or organizing it according to his own prejudices. While the degree of form or structure varies with each phenomenon, no phenomenon of life whether animate or inanimate appears to the individual as completely devoid of order. Each reflects a time, space, or logical order. Such form or structure or order is, of course, an inherent and important part of the phenomenon of communication, from the most basic sequence of introduction, body, and conclusion to the more sophisticated concerns of the sequence of ideas within these basic parts.

One who spends his life haphazardly gathering impressions, opinions, and facts and who communicates them in the same way they were gathered is like a builder who spends years gathering all sorts of exotic and special materials for construction of a mighty building but never attempts to arrange them in an order which will insure strength, beauty, or convenience. It is not enough to select and gather materials for communication. They must be ordered and used as the occasion demands.

In oral communication, even more than in written communication, order plays an important role in deciding the degree of success or failure. In the instances where individual words fail to convey a clear meaning to the listener, for example, a knowledge of the larger order or design of the speaker helps. Such knowledge comes, first of all, from the order of the sentence in which the word is placed. Meaning is revealed by each word's association with other words which perform certain functions in the sentence. Thus, "red" by itself means several things; in the sentence "John is a red," its meaning is more precisely prescribed. Further, the meaning of individual words is indicated by the position and function played by the sentence in the larger unit, the paragraph. In this way, we are able to deduce the meanings of words used inaccurately or ambiguously by children, foreigners, the uneducated, and even the careless speaker.

The order or design of a speaker's message is revealed most obviously by his own description of it before and during his act of communication. Thus, if a speaker says he will discuss the impact of the aerospace industry on the nation, the community, and the individual citizen, the listener "sets" himself to receive information in each of these areas and in this sequence. Less obviously, the speaker's design is revealed by the sequence of his discussion, the time and place in which it is given, and by a knowledge of the events leading up to the communication. As parents, by way of example, we note from the initial comments of flattery and from the unusual concern for our welfare that our children will soon request favors. As executives, we assume that a meeting arranged by a representative of labor just prior to the expiration of a contract will be concerned—even indirectly—with the present and future conditions of the contract.

In most instances of oral communication, two major types of order function most effectively and these are best revealed in the development of the selected themes. These basic forms of reason include *deduction* which is a movement from general concepts (of time, order, or other associations) to specific instances, and *induction* which involves a logical movement from specific instances to general categories related to those instances.

DEVELOPMENT

Having clearly defined and limited his topic, then having selected the relevant subpoints, the speaker must now move to select a method of demonstrating the connection between various subpoints and between the subpoints and the main points which make up his theme. Without abandoning the main idea, he must summon other ideas which will confirm, strengthen, and clarify it. Held together by the main ideas, the supporting illustrations and examples form a meaningful pattern. Without such a clear relationship, without a logical association, the main ideas and supporting examples used by a speaker represent little more than a meaningless jumble much like the beads of a broken necklace. Simply stated, an effective communicator is able to give reasons for his statements and his actions.

The logical association referred to as *deduction* is most generally identified or demonstrated through the use of a syllogism, or an argument which has three closely interrelated parts. Thus, one might argue:

>All Italians are hot-tempered
>Mario is an Italian
>Therefore, Mario is hot-tempered.

However, no one speaks *habitually* in syllogistic fashion and very few *ever* speak in this way.[1] As an artificial device (invented by Aristotle) constructed to *test* some of the more formal types of oral communication, it achieved great popularity. Unfortunately, its identity as a test was lost in the surge of popularity and it soon became a part of the material taught to students of speech as an ideal form of communication. This is obviously a serious mistake since, once away from the classroom, the student soon learns of its impractical qualities and drops it from further consideration of any kind. *It should be learned, but only as a test to be applied to the real form* of deduction used in oral communication: the enthymeme.[2]

The enthymeme is a kind of syllogism. It is frequently used in communication and generally takes the form of a conclusion welded to a statement from which the conclusion came. Thus, "If he has never played baseball, he is not an American." The conclusion ("he is not an American") is offered because of the earlier observation ("if he has never played baseball") plus an unstated belief ("All Americans play baseball"). Other examples demonstrate the same *assumed connection*:

Blessed are the meek, for they shall inherit the earth.	Conclusion: Blessed are the meek. Because: They (the meek) shall inherit the earth. Unstated: All who inherit the earth are blessed.
Someone must have died because the flag is at half-mast.	Conclusion: Someone must have died. Because: The flag is at half-mast. Unstated: Whenever someone dies the flag is put at half-mast.

The possibility of error, of drawing false conclusions, becomes more obvious when the enthymeme *is restated to include the unstated assumptions*. When exceptions are drawn up for the statements and when the connections between statements are tested to determine whether it shows what it purports to show, the concept is properly tested.

The oral communicator who is serious about improving his ability to communicate effectively would do well to apply the basic test suggested by the previous discussion; he would do very well to apply it *when he assembles his materials as a speaker* and when he, as a listener, *receives the materials assembled by another speaker.*

Closely allied to the matter of deduction (usually observed as enthymemes in oral conversation) is the *inductive* mode of logical association. This, as noted earlier, is the process of piling one instance upon another

---

1. John Locke, *An Essay Concerning Human Understanding,* Book IV, selected by Mary W. Calkins (LaSalle, Ill.: The Open Court Publishing Company, 1949), p. 267.
2. Most generally pronounced *en-the-meem*.

until an obvious conclusion is forthcoming. Its most perfect form is complete enumeration—a one hundred percent listing of instances, a perfect survey omitting not one single example. As with the syllogism of the deductive form of reasoning, the perfect enumeration is rarely if ever a part of inductive reasoning as applied to oral communication. Rather, induction is most commonly identified as the example or the analogy.

Thus, one hears reasoning when he hears, "I think the Bramas will win the league championship since they have won it every year for the last ten years." So, too, in the situation where he hears, "Those students at Tukwila University are not to be trusted since those two cheating scandals came out." Testing this form of reasoning amounts to finding exceptions in the same materials used by the speaker (other years when the Bramas did *not* win; known students from Tukwila University who did *not* cheat) or by noting that the examples used for the conclusion were not typical.

The analogy is thought to be literal if it is based upon some actual example, or figurative if based upon some hypothetical relationship defined by the speaker. Either way, it is an indirect way of concluding something from prior experience; it assumes similar results will follow similar causes in situations which are quite similar. Thus, if one got hives twice after eating crabmeat, he would probably avoid crabmeat. When he moves to avoid shrimp as well, he gives evidence of reasoning by analogy. He moved from defining a series of likenesses between two things and an unpleasant experience associated with one of them, *to the conclusion* that the second thing will also produce unpleasantness. Notice that, while this movement of thought shows many possibilities for error, it is not as gross as a movement which would go from crabmeat to all edible things.

The main weakness with this type of reasoning is that as the similarities became fewer and more indirect, the argument gets proportionally weaker. Argument by analogy always assumes there are more similarities than dissimilarities or that similarities are more important than dissimilarities. Very often, a few similar but unimportant theses are offered as evidence for a conclusion, when the actual value of a conclusion depends on theses not stated.

The inductive mode, then, attempts to abstract from similar details in each instance and infer a generalization.

It should be evident, even at this point in the discussion, that the speaker's message carries probative force or persuasive power by its clarity and logical development. It should be clear, also, that the core of human reasoning is made up of fact and inferences drawn from other facts. These inferences may be drawn by induction or deduction but, however they are arrived at, it is important that the connecting threads be strong, direct, and intact. In proportion as they are, and are demonstrated, the listener will more readily understand and accept the conclusion.

Oddly enough, we pretend to demand logic in others, but rarely do we examine the soundness of our own conclusions. For this reason, arguments which are most purely logical, that is, quite obvious in their logical relationships, often tend to be put aside since the contrast between what the listener hears and what he knows he offers, casts an unfavorable light upon himself. The myth that "man is a logical animal" was started by man. More a hope than a fact, this myth has served to confound as much as to help. More truthfully, man is an animal capable of *both* rational and nonrational activity. Relation of logical and psychological materials is always tenuous. That the coexistence of both categories stands in the most intelligent persons has long been established. Superstitious scientists, fanatically religious college professors, prejudiced judges and the like, substantiate the existence of this phenomenon. Society schools its young in the hope that the logical will dominate the illogical—most of the time. Should the reverse occur, the individual is segregated formally by commitment to an institution or informally by ostracism from the various circles of society.

Reason alone has rarely influenced anyone. "The facts," if they could be universally accepted, would always need some motivating agent to make them palatable to a certain audience at a certain time. If reason alone were sufficent, then we would need no schools, churches, industries, and so forth; a mere citation of the facts would lead to the only possible conclusion. But even with the same set of facts, men arrive at different conclusions. The smoker and nonsmoker, Supreme Court Justices and attorneys, the drinker and nondrinker, the Catholic and Protestant, the Chevron customer and the Shell customer do not disagree on matters of fact. They disagree, rather, on the conclusions drawn from those facts, or on matters not even a part of any related experience.

It has long been true of human activity that the "logical proposes and the psychological disposes." No sooner does the listener catch the speaker's *psychological* emphases—to share his likes, dislikes, indignations and joys—than he assumes the speaker's point of view. Psychological motivations—appeals to hopes, fears, desires, prejudices—have rarely caused a lasting persuasion when operating alone. "Nothing," we are reminded by the European adage, "is so rapid as the drying of a teardrop; nothing so transient as states of bliss." Nevertheless, such appeals used wisely have caused great refinement in the actions of men. Few people have ever been persuaded to pursue a certain course of action or to abandon another without having that action related to gratification of some need. Whether it is done because it is honorable or good or profitable or necessary, it is done because it fulfills that particular need experienced by the listener. One such need, little appreciated by many scholars of democratic societies, is the need to rely on *authority*.[3]

As has been pointed out, dependence upon authority increases as the society becomes more complex; the more removed the average person is from original experiences, the more he depends upon the experience of others. No man can live long enough to acquire by direct experience all of the needed information to operate efficiently in today's world; more importantly, few live long enough to understand such information. To develop as rational social beings, men become indebted to others for everything about the past and for most things concerning the present. Few of us have directly experienced certain aspects of farming, warfare, space flight, travel to Russia, medical advancement, and the like. None of us personally knew Jesus, Columbus, or George Washington, yet because of the testimony of others, we operate as though we did. Anyone we feel indebted to is treated as an authority. If enough persons are indebted to the same person, he becomes an expert.

The importance of authority in everyday activity is significant even in the most democratic societies. The relationship of child to parent, student to teacher, worker to boss, and citizen to administrator demonstrates the role and influence of authority in our lives. There is an evident role played by testimonials in selling everything from religion to cigarettes. Generally speaking, it is more difficult for the average listener to reject a proposition, plan, or program when it comes to him clearly, when it is in language which is meaningful, and when it bears the stamp of approval from someone highly respected and admired. Ideas rarely have force standing alone. They are believed or disbelieved only when they are advanced by an individual or an institution. The power value of ideas, therefore, is partially determined by the authorities supporting them.

Another significant but not generally recognized need, is that which causes most listeners to seek out and believe those things for which they already carry *conviction*. And, accordingly, they seem to expect the same from others, particularly of a speaker who wishes to claim a portion of their time, money, or effort. Ministers who reveal that they would rather be playing golf than delivering "the same old message," doctors who, while inhaling a cigarette, try to convince patients that smoking is bad for the health, teachers who discourse on the value of personal conferences with students while never arranging them for their own students, all demonstrate a certain lack of conviction which the sensitive auditor finds difficult to ignore. Few persons would be willing to accept the adage "Do as I

---

3. H. Gilkinson, S. Paulson, D. Sikkink, "Effects of Order and Authority in An Argumentative Speech," *Quarterly Journal of Speech* XL (April, 1954), pp. 183-192.

say not as I do," particularly when it accompanies urgent pleas on important matters.

A speaker wishing to be effective will recognize the importance of his own convictions in any of his attempts to move others toward understanding or action. Equivocation, excessive modification and the like generally serve to confuse and confound the listener. Few things are more objectionable to an audience than a good idea associated with a mediocre speaker. On the other hand, a seemingly mediocre idea assumes other proportions when offered by a speaker convinced of its worth and ready to describe this worth to the listener. False enthusiasm will rarely survive as a moving force with extended exposure before sensitive listeners. People are not inclined to share their time with others who seem to believe one thing but who speak on another. On occasion, the wise speaker makes a decision not to talk with a certain group at a certain time on a certain subject because of his own lack of conviction and closeness to the ideas, programs, or policies.

In addition to such psychological aids as authority and conviction, the speaker can add to the value of his message by efficacious *humor*. Aside from visual aids, the most misused of the speaker's forces is humor. Properly employed, humor can make the difference between a communication which is lived and one which is endured.

It is now commonplace among experts that the essence of humor is incongruity; it is the revelation of the unexpected. In the clash of two incongruities, there appears what has been called "the flash of humor." These incongruities may be in matters of time, form, and substance related to people, places, things, events, *and the relationships among these*. But all individuals are not equal in their ability to detect the existence of incongruity or to appreciate the resultant "flash" emerging from a confrontation of two incongruities. For this reason, some people are thought of as being devoid of a sense of humor; others are labeled as highly sensitive to humor. For this reason, also, there are various levels of humor.

The most basic form of humor, appreciated by all but the most common among the primitive tribes and the uneducated in modern society, is that demonstrated by physical incongruity. The man who walks with a gait not common to most individuals, the fat woman who tries to sit on a small stool, the person sporting a pie on his face, all these situations can be recognized and appreciated as humor by the most uncultivated mind. The more sophisticated level of humor is that which involves less direct behavior and more symbolic concerns. As an individual or a society becomes more cultured, as either begins to substitute symbolic processes for the direct processes wherever possible, appreciation of verbal humor is made more real. The ironical or sarcastic, a pun, quip, or story represent the refined development of the more sophisticated level of humor.

A sense of humor has often been looked on as an infallible sign of a healthy personality. Whether or not this is true, men believe their fellows reveal the extent of their mental and emotional flexibility through habitual patterns of humor. They appear to single out the individual who is capable of noting certain subtle relationships, has the willingness to remove himself from immersion in the immediate situation, and can appreciate the build-up of tension required for the recognition of the "flash" which designates true humor. The oral communicator exercising control over himself and certain aspects of his environment helps to create for his listener a special and brief moment of truth. This he does by working artistically with the materials *in the immediate communicative situation* to arrange for the juxtaposition of two or more incongruities. Then, allowing the listener only bits and pieces of this arrangement through a gradual unfolding process, the speaker suddenly and precisely reveals the "flash" of complete vision, and humor is experienced.

This ability has benefits for both the individual and his society. From the standpoint of the individual, it enables him to achieve the perspective necessary to a better understanding of any event, person, institution, or process.[4] When one sees the humorous aspect of these things, it is as though he has seen the dark side of the moon and thus a deeper appreciation of its true nature. The most obvious case in point is the person who can see humor in some of his own thoughts, attitudes, and actions. Armed with this insight, he can maintain balance in his relationships and worth in his activities; equipped with a sense of discernment, he provides himself with the priceless medicine for physical pain and mental torment. And so with the society which fosters and values humor. Throughout history the remark has been made that without the ability to laugh at itself, a society is doomed to an early death. When jokes cease to be made, when laughter is no longer heard, and when the list of subjects considered to be above humor continues to grow, concern for the life of society arises. Whether in individuals or societies, humor is most troublesome to the insecure and the ill.

But as with medicine, humor can be misapplied. It can be rendered useless (and sometimes harmful) because of the person using it, the patient to whom it is applied, or the time, place, and circumstance of application. The respected oral communicator recognizes the difference between *planned* and *spontaneous* humor. Planned humor, whether in nonverbal form (dress, posture, gait, practical jokes, etc.) or in the verbal mode (stories and puns), has the advantage of control and places less strain on the speaker. On the other hand, planned humor is disadvanta-

---

4. See John G. Fuller's column "Trade Winds," *The Saturday Review* (July 16, 1966), pp. 16-17. Also Evan Esar, *The Humor of Humor* (New York: Horizon Press, 1952), pp. 7-11.

Skills of the Speaker: Message Analysis 77

geous in most communicative situations because it is dated and carries an air of mechanization and remoteness which weakens its psychological value. Spontaneous humor, by contrast, has the greater psychological benefit because it is more fluid, dynamic, timely, and personal. And yet, these are the very qualities which increase the speaker's chance of failure since all persons are not equally proficient in its use.

Generally speaking, speakers should avoid the canned story—particularly at the introduction. Contrary to popular opinion, there is no evidence to support the contention that it "gets the audience with you." As has been noted by the first principle discussed in Chapter 2, good communication is organized, meaningful, and selectively particular. Most story jokes fulfill none of these qualities since, by their very nature, they relate to other times and other circumstances. Unless the speaker can make the relationship between the story and *all factors of the immediate situation* (listener, time, place, message, speaker) he should avoid its use. Effective adaptation can be made, but as with other matters of consequence, it requires sensitivity, care, and precision.

Adaptation of stories begins, of course, by changing names, places, dates, and actions so that they come within the experience of the immediate listener. For example, in telling the well-known joke involving a sly dig, the following possibilities exist:

Do you know that the brains of —— { secretaries / doctors / lawyers / ministers / executives } sell to researchers for as much as $10.00 a pound while those gotten from _____ cost as much as $25.00 a pound?

Depending upon his audience, the speaker can inject the name of any group he wishes into the blank spots to secure maximum results. Thus, if speaking to educators, he might well inject *principal* or *dean* or *superintendent*. He would, accordingly, alter the first list to avoid mentioning the group reserved for the punch line which is, (in answer to the inevitable question WHY), "Do you know how many _____ it takes to get a pound of brains?" Similarly, one may alter the various phrases and sequence of phrases to suit his particular need. Note how one joke can be made to suit different listeners, occasions, and so on.

I can't remember the name but the { language / breath / pain / aggressiveness / boredom / dogma } is familiar.

If one were speaking to an appreciative minister, rabbi, priest, or nun, he could easily insert the word *faith* for a good "play" on the original version.

                                a group or profession
Do you know it takes 5 (*being joked about*   ) to replace a light bulb—one to hold the bulb and four to turn the ladder?

With all the possibilities for modification and adaptation of standard stories, the strongest type of humor remains the pun, quip, reversed proverb, or story drawn from the immediate environment. The speech professor who, after hearing a long and embarrassing introduction about his achievements and prowess as a speaker, starts by saying, "Unaccustomed as I am to public speaking" does just that sort of thing. So does the speaker who capitalizes upon accidents, noises, and other distractions which occur during his presentation. But proficiency does not come simply by wishing; one must understand the importance of *timing* (adequate pausing and phrasing), *adaptation,* and *practice* in this as in other aspects of the communicative process.

At an earlier point, the thought was expressed that people are influenced by their ability to understand and by their decisions to act because of the force brought upon them by the speaker, the message, and the occasion. In terms of the message, it has been suggested that its force is carried by clarity, development, and style. Having considered the pertinent parts of both clarity and development, the conscientious speaker moves to understand the intricacies of style or the proficient use of language.

STYLE

Effective use of language adds unquestioned force to the message and most of all to clarity. The words selected, the arrangement of these words, and the artistic consideration of specialized functions of the various arrangements all contribute to make the message confused or clear, weak, or forceful. The use of one type of language throughout an extended talk inevitably results in monotony and destroys the listener's interest and capacity to profit from the communication. Long and involved sentence structure unrelieved by colloquial language soon becomes tiresome; excessive slang also fatigues the mind and encourages it to wander. A linguistic style saturated with variety is deadly; a linguistic style so variable as to be inconsistent is bewildering. *One who sincerely wishes to communicate with another will construct a style which points as directly as possible to the idea or the feeling being expressed and nothing else.* He begins the construction by attending to his basic building material: words.

Words

As wonderful as speech is, it represents an attempt to make static that which is dynamic, to section off a part of a continuous panorama of experiences which are in the process of developing. As a fluid assumes the shape of its container, ideas and experiences take on the qualities of the pre-existing words used to describe them. By using words, one categorizes and in so doing removes or minimizes the unique features of the concepts or feelings. For this reason, the careful communicator works continually for a better appreciation of the words in his vocabulary and those available to him in the vocabulary of his society. The English speaking communities have well over one-half million words available to them, and as society progresses into new areas with new experiences, that number will increase. The average individual within these communities has a vocabulary of approximately ten thousand words and of these uses about two thousand in his habitual patterns of conversation. Difficulty arises because of the misuse of some words and the overuse of others.

The efficient speaker is aware that English provides him with some words which are *general* (designating classes of things or activities such as animal, fish, sports, etc.); some which are *specific* (designating units within the general classes such as dog, salmon, baseball, etc.); some which are *abstract* (designating qualities or states which exist nowhere but in the minds of the communicants such as righteous, republicanism, love, etc.); and others which are *concrete* (designating things and actions which can be and are regularly experienced such as boyhood, school, marriage, etc.). Even more helpful is the speaker's realization that whether general or specific, abstract or concrete words vary in their meanings according to the speaker, listener, time, place, and the occasion associated with their use.

All words, in order to be included in the vocabulary of any society, must have (or have had) a *denotation,* that is, a meaning which many (or most) of the people in the society share with reasonable limits. In many societies, such meanings are noted in dictionaries which are compiled to record usage; they are not used to set standards. Thus, a stranger, or younger or relatively uneducated member in a society will put himself closer to his contemporaries by referring to the dictionary whenever he is unsure how a word is used. And so will the educated person profit, for meanings—even denotations—are in a constant state of flux. It can readily be seen that a speaker using the word *compact* must differentiate in its use much more carefully today than if he were speaking in 1945; an elderly person using *dashboard* to a teen-ager must be certain that the younger man shares his image of a place against which one places his foot when the horses start galloping with the carriage. In a few years, it is conceivable that some children may have to resort to the dictionary to find out what their grandparents mean when they speak of a *cow*. To make matters even more difficult, because many people have such imprecise denotations to begin with, only a very careful reexamination will bring them to their attention. Efficient communication is not possible without precise denotations of words. What, if any, is the difference in denotation between *aggravate* and *irritate, best* and *better, liberal* and *free, love* and *like*? Could these differences really alter understanding?

But even if the denotation of a word were sharp and clear to both speaker and listener, misunderstanding could still arise from the cloud of social and/or personal associations *(connotations)* trailing after it. If these associations are strong enough, the denotation is lost in a haze of specialized meanings which the speaker intends but the listener misses, or which the listener appends to what the speaker intends. Either way, the participants in the communicative situation are being driven apart while, on the surface, they appear to be intimate companions in thought. A somewhat detailed account of one such instance must answer for the thousands of others which occur daily. Suppose a speaker were addressing an audience of Christian religious workers on the subject of communication and, particularly, on the three aspects of life which are brought to bear by any speaker: experience, training, and research. In approaching this point he could introduce it with the following:

> A speaker's efficiency is determined by his use of a trinity composed of experience, training, and research.

Obviously, the use of the word *trinity* is perfectly in order since its denotation is tripart, triad, or anything else representing an amalgamation of three discrete entities. But before this particular audience, the speaker would be ill-advised to use such a word *because of the cloud* (or halo) *of religious associations which the listeners share* and which are completely apart from the legitimate meaning. On the other hand, if he were speaking to an audience composed of atheists, Moslems, or even a cross section of the world's population, his choice of *trinity* instead of a synonym would not be as hazardous. In less dramatic situations, the word *biweekly* could present as many confusions. Unless the speaker clearly differentiates between twice a week or once every two weeks, the listener might think one when the speaker intends the other.

In sum, the good speaker will make a definite word judgment in each instance of his oral communicative experiences. And such a judgment will always be made in terms of the propriety and effectiveness as *defined by the listener and the circumstances of the occasion*—not according to the speaker's experience.

Composition

The art of putting words together into meaningful patterns is referred to as composition. Here again, the good communicator is aware of the importance of order. Taken separately, words, like the pieces of a mosaic, are of minor interest only. After revealing their color and form, they cease to function. If, however, they are combined by a skilled person, they can produce a wonderful masterpiece. Handled by an unskilled person, they can only form a combination or grouping which is naïve, confusing, or with little meaning. The words cannot be pronounced in random fashion and still convey the speaker's ideas to the listener. In beginning societies, the accepted practice was to pronounce the most important parts of the idea first and follow these with the accessories. As ideas, subtle relationships of activity and refinements of feeling develop, more precise associations are demanded. The result is grammar. The natural order presents words in succession according to the desires of the speaker. The grammatical order presents words according to the relationship which they bear to each other. Thus, one order is specific and concerned only with the immediate idea being expressed and the other order is more general and is concerned with all ideas. It is important that every member of a speaking community knows enough of the basic rules of the game (and language is a game played according to rules previously agreed upon and not subject to immediate change) to avoid blunders which will encourage confusion and possible tragedy.

If the purpose of language is to convey thought or feeling, then whatever interferes with that purpose should be eliminated and whatever enhances it should be developed. In addition to having concern for basic rules of grammar, the effective speaker is aware of the length and complexity of his sentences. Since the listener cannot refer to what was said as easily as a reader can, and since the listener tends to be easily distracted when listening, the speaker must make certain his ideas are immediately intelligible. Proper words, well arranged, help to create this immediate intelligibility; short, uninvolved sentences help insure it. In oral practice, sentences from ten to twenty words long prove to be most effective. A common failing is to use sentences which are too long and to use a written rather than oral style. Too many words, too many clauses, too many parenthetical expressions, and too many transitions are all communication barriers.

For purposes of variety, effective speakers endeavor to mix the two most basic forms of the sentence, the *periodic* and the *loose*. The periodic sentence presents the essentials of the idea at the end of its construction. The loose sentence, on the other hand, presents the essentials of the idea at the beginning of its construction and follows with the necessary modifiers. For example, note the samples:

Periodic	Loose
On a lonely road, in the middle of the night, one cold evening in December, *John was killed*.	*John was killed,* on a lonely road, in the middle of the night, one cold evening in December.
In an instance of this sort, without further thought, *Stafford should sue*.	*Stafford should sue,* in an instance of this sort, without further thought.

It can easily be seen that there are advantages to each form. The periodic arrangement is best for establishing a suspension of attention, for the marshalling of thoughts, for added emphasis. The loose structure is best for bringing matters to the fore more rapidly. It should be remembered that children, older persons, and those more easily fatigued require shorter more direct sentences. But all audiences must have these sentences used in combination.

Linguistic Devices

For the most effective style, *variety* is indispensable. Periodic sentences mixed with loose sentences, comparisons mixed with contrasts, negations mixed with positive sentences, complex ideas interspersed with simple thoughts, all add to the individual speaker's force and effectiveness. Part of this variety, part of the ultimate sense of force is contributed to by figurative language. Wisely employed, figurative language is fresh, novel, and serves to explain, illustrate, and enforce ideas.

Unfortunately, figurative language is often considered too remote from natural speech to be of much use. Yet, this is precisely the language used in the course of everyday communication. Because people learn best by having an unknown thought, feeling, or activity associated with one they already know about, figurative language (which provides a diagram for such associations) is readily accepted. This is especially true when one seeks to communicate about nonphysical matters, about matters of the mind. We begin, usually, by noting that the unknown object, idea, or relationship is actually much like something we have already experienced. Thus, a companion is born.

Figurative language is generally classified according to the type of association it stresses. There are examples which stress *resemblance,* those which emphasize *contiguity* of time or space, and those which stress the idea of *contrast*.[5]

---

5. Note the unusual flavor added to a concept when one uses the linguistic device of the oxymoron to emphasize contrast: economic luxury, cold heat, planned casualness, frenzied relaxation, bright darkness, etc.

Skills of the Speaker: Message Analysis

One of the most common figures and one of the easiest to use is *simile.* It is a direct attempt to relate two things of different classes by actually saying they are related. It is the portrait of a painter. In making the statement, words such as *like, as, similar to* and *resembling* are used as bridges. Thus, drawn from popular speech, we commonly hear: "good as gold," "sharp as a tack," and so forth. Similes are designed to clarify and enforce ideas though the effect is less than is provided for by metaphors.

The *metaphor* expresses a strong and direct link between things of a different class. It does not create a bridge; instead, *it makes the two things as one,* thereby creating a stronger bond. It is the portrait of a mirror. Notice the difference between the following pairs: John swims like a fish versus John is a fish; The Lord is like my shepherd versus The Lord is my shepherd. Thus, the metaphor aids understanding and produces a style of brevity and freshness.

Other forceful figures include *understatement* and *parallelism.* The former, by opposing the popular tendency toward exaggeration, calls itself to the listener's attention forcefully. The latter clarifies and strengthens by offering ideas in balanced form whether between sections of a talk, between sentences, or within the same sentence. So, one feels the impact of "cry if you must, yell if you wish, protest if it pleases you."

As with all other aspects of good thought and language, the best figures spring naturally out of the subject, the time, and place and are varied enough to prevent boredom, confusion, or monotony.

SUMMARY

Good speakers strive to make their messages clear and orderly by carefully blending logical and psychological approaches. The style of the message, including proper and sensitive use of words, sentence arrangement, and linguistic devices, does affect listeners.

PRACTICAL REMINDERS

Propositions

1. Clearly organized communication is more helpful in directing listeners toward acceptance of the speaker's message than that which is not.
2. The specific order of the ideas presented must vary with the listener, time, place, and circumstance.
3. Generally speaking, it is best to place the weakest arguments in between stronger ones so the speaker begins and ends on strong points.
4. Enthymemes are more common to effective oral communication than syllogisms.

5. Messages which fill a clearly defined need in the speaker will be more readily accepted than those which do not.

6. Messages which include evidence for the general conclusions are more acceptable than those which do not.

7. Messages which demonstrate the support of authorities well known and respected by the listeners will be more effective than those which do not.

8. Messages which have conclusions explicitly stated by the speaker are generally more effective than those which have not.

9. Messages which make frequent use of simple transitions (first, second, another important cause is, etc.) are more effective than those which do not.

10. Humor is most effective when it is drawn from the specific audience and occasion. "Set" stories and jokes are less effective, but may be improved by adaptation to the audience and occasion.

11. No effective speaker seeks to cultivate one style to suit all occasions.

12. Messages are strengthened by effective use of metaphor, understatement, and parallelism.

Exercises

Theme

Directions: In each of the following examples, the subject as stated by the speaker confuses rather than clarifies the listener's initial understanding. Write your improved version in the space provided opposite each example.

1. Democracy is the best form of government.
2. The American way of life is ideal.
3. Brotherhood is the key to social living.

1.
2.
3.

Order

A. *Directions*: Refinement and precision of thought are best demonstrated by the nature and extent of the sequences, categories, and other relationships provided by the speaker.

Arrange the following names into as many groups as you can logically support:

Sammy Davis, Jr., Dwight D. Eisenhower, John F. Kennedy, Frank Sinatra, Joe E. Lewis, Albert Schweitzer, William Howard Taft, Nat King Cole, John Barrymore,

Skills of the Speaker: Message Analysis

Primo Carnera, Galileo Galilei, Jonas Salk, Malcolm X, John Unitas, Jim Thorpe.

B. *Directions*: From the following list, select those words which are generic and those which are specific. Develop a plan which demonstrates the relationship of the words in each section.
   1. addition, nevertheless, and, but, also, contrast, thus, furthermore, summary, in fine, hence, moreover, so, consequently
   2. creeping, theft, lying, riding, running, crime, sound, singing, robbery, motion, groaning

C. *Directions*: Can you rearrange the following statements into an acceptable outline, i.e., one which reflects coordination, subordination, discreteness, proper symbolization, and indentation?
   1. The Orpet trial in Waukegan, Illinois cost $30,000.
   2. As citizens, you are subject to serve on jury duty.
   3. The present system of trial by jury should be replaced.
   4. The present systems lack certainty.
   5. The present system is obsolete according to the needs of this age.
   6. Judge Medina estimated that a recent trial in New York cost the taxpayers $100,000.
   7. Juror qualifications are too general.
   8. As defendant, you may have to depend upon a jury's efficiency.
   9. Jurors must rely upon memory regardless of the length of the trial.
   10. The method of selecting jurors is antiquated.
   11. Unprejudiced jurors are nonexistent in our society.
   12. Jurors often vary in their interpretation of the same evidence.
   13. Verdicts are often contrary to the evidence available.
   14. The method of taking, recording, and evaluating evidence is inefficient.
   15. The jury system has a direct effect upon you.
   16. Histrionics of opposing counsels often impede objective judgment by jurors.

Development

Directions: Test these enthymemes by providing the *unstated* portion of the thought.
   1. I will pass the exam today because I have my lucky pen with me.
   2. The Protestant religion should be abandoned since doctrinal unity is not possible.
   3. I am a veteran, why must I work?

4. That team will lose the game because it has thirteen members on the squad.

Words

A. *Directions*: Make a record of the denotation of each word listed below. Note particularly how the denotation prevents confusion with a similar word.

1. aggravate — irritate
2. preservation — conservation
3. pestilence — disease
4. funny — odd
5. invent — discover
6. journey — walk
7. infer — imply
8. test — examine

B. *Directions*: Place the stress mark (′) in the appropriate place to distinguish between the following pairs.

1. instinct — instinct
2. conflict — conflict
3. converse — converse
4. compress — compress
5. essay — essay
6. refuse — refuse
7. record — record
8. permit — permit

Composition

A. *Directions*: Rewrite each of the following sentences to alleviate the ambiguity.

1. While asleep, the service station manager discovered the employee and fired him.
    (Who is asleep?)
2. Julius and Ida have been planning a trip to Italy for two years.
    (Long trip or bad planning?)
3. Heavy ladies' sweaters, $18.95.
    (None for slim ladies?)
4. Pat was elected Queen and escorted to the festival by Granny.
    (Who elected her?)
5. The Boys' Club has a director, two gyms with libraries and restrooms.
    (Strange arrangements?)

B. *Directions*: Complete the following similes so you construct a new and clear understanding. Avoid Clichés.

1. As nervous as _____
2. As quiet as _____
3. As cool as _____
4. As obnoxious as _____
5. As stupid as _____
6. As talkative as _____
7. As generous as _____
8. As faithful as _____
9. As foolish as _____
10. As good as _____

C. *Directions*: Some of the following linguistic devices are useless because their various parts are inconsistent with each other and they serve to create a confused image. Identify the following poor examples and rewrite them in correct form.

1. He reported that the backbone of the cold wave was broken.
2. Each employee is an active member of the mosaic of our company.
3. Fred is an important arm in the administrative chain of this company.
4. Al's always stepping on the toes of the channels of authority.
5. He made as much impact as a dewdrop falling on a sponge.
6. The waves of indignation, stitched by the actions of a few, went like a shot through the audience.
7. He liked to work and taking in movies.
8. Ted not only found an employee but also a friend.
9. His pay as retail clerk is much higher than a truck driver.
10. Marie's eyes are dark like a cow.

Readings

Arnold, Carroll C. "Reader or Listener? Oral Composition." *Today's Speech*, February 1, 1965, pp. 5-7.

Ayer, Alfred Jules. *Language, Truth and Logic*. New York: Dover Publications, Inc., 1946.

Brennan, Lawrence. *Modern Communication Effectiveness*. Englewood Cliffs, N. J.: Prentice-Hall, Inc., 1963.

Cassirer, E. *The Philosophy of Symbolic Forms*. New Haven: Yale University Press, 1953-57, (3 Volumes).

Hoch, P., and Zubin, J. eds. *Psychopathology of Communication*. New York: Grune & Stratton, 1958.

Pei, M. *The Story of Language*. New York: Mentor Books, 1949.

Postman, N., et al, eds. *Language in America*. New York: Pegasus, 1969.

Wiener, M., and Mehrabian, A. *Language Within Language: Immediacy, A Channel in Verbal Communication*. New York: Appleton-Century-Crofts, 1968.

Chapter 5

SKILLS OF THE SPEAKER—SITUATION ANALYSIS

Among many educators and lay persons there is a belief that time, place, and circumstance have slight effect on persuasion or learning. Others feel the only thing that matters in persuasion or learning is where and when it occurs. Both positions are seriously overstated, but are contained in the earlier statement of Principle A:[1] The dynamics of oral communication result from the psychophysical aspects of the immediate environment.

From the general experience of living, most people realize that the psychophysical environment does play a significant part in shaping such things as attitudes, attention, and memory. It is easy enough to recall the feelings when, as an adult, one walked into a schoolroom, a church, or a country club. The feelings are not similar. Some bring back certain attitudes and expectations not a part of other environments.

Depth, color, and width are often added to a message as a result of where and when the speaker chooses to deliver it. Often these added dimensions are strong enough to change the original evaluation of the message while at other times they serve to add strength to the original choice. Think, for example, of the possible reactions to a message which the listener discovers has never been delivered before ("I love you"), or has been delivered regularly by the same person to many audiences ("You are the best class I have ever had"), or is always delivered at a certain time and place by different speakers (exhortations by commencement speakers). Is not the metamessage in each instance different? Do not some bits of information detract while some add to the message?

One of the more important of the physical factors which influences listener reaction is *time*. Quite apart from the element of time which considers the immediate psychological state of both speaker and listener from the most informal communication (a pleasant "hello" immediately upon

1. See Chapter 2.

rising in the morning as opposed to no comment at all) to the more formal classroom situations (conferences and seminars), the impact of time helps or hinders the success of the activity. Among adult professionals, for example, most successful conferences appear to be held in the autumn months while those in the spring and winter tend to be less successful. This does not mean, of course, that successful conferences cannot be organized for summer months; it does mean that summer imposes more obstacles to success than other seasons of the year, and the successful communicator must do something to overcome them. Is not this the feeling regarding school sessions? While there are many successful summer schools, students seem to do better in the learning situations organized during the other months. The more informal communications do not appear to be as affected, although there is some reason to believe that even these ought to be conducted with an eye toward the impact of shorter attention span, ease of distraction, and the like.

In like manner, it has been found that Tuesday, Wednesday, or Thursday are better days for the more formal, complex, or important communications. So, too, with the various hours of the day. People tend to be more alert, interested, and motivated during the early morning and afternoon hours. Speakers should base their choice of time more on concern for listener capacities than on personal convenience. The best time appears to be from nine to eleven-thirty in the morning and two to four-thirty in the afternoon. If evening sessions must be held, seven-thirty to nine-thirty proves most profitable. These times allow the listener greater freedom from such natural handicaps as fatigue, hunger, and boredom. It seems most unwise for a distraught husband to attempt a successful communication with his wife between five and six-thirty, particularly if he wishes a decision on whether they should accept a transfer to another town. Tired as he is, he must recognize the barriers of fatigue (she, too, is probably feeling the adverse effects of being active for nine hours) and distraction (getting dinner, small children underfoot) which automatically work against his success. It would be far better to wait until dinner is over, the dishes are put away and the children are in bed. An executive who calls a meeting for four-thirty on Friday afternoon must do much more to neutralize natural barriers than one who consults with his people between two and four on Thursday. The teacher who chooses to hold his classes during the noon hour must exert more profound and constant judgments than one who selects an hour free from inherent competitions. And so it is with all instances of communication. If it is to be successful, a communion, no matter how fleeting or important, should be held during those moments which the speaker knows to be ideal.

Finally, the good speaker must consider the influence of time in terms of the length of his communication. Considering the speaker, listener, subject, and circumstance, should the message be five minutes in length? Ten? Forty? Indefinite? At times the length of the communicative experience cannot be predetermined. One hardly knows beforehand how long it will take to persuade a friend to accompany him to a ball game. On the other hand, the teacher knows that a specific class session can be only fifty or thirty or forty-five minutes long and he endeavors to work successfully within these artificial controls. Generally speaking, both communicators exemplified above would do well to remember the greater number of barriers imposed by longer messages. Since most people have untrained memories, are easily distracted and cannot follow long chains of reasoning, the speaker would do well to shape shorter messages which are both direct and simple. Messages which run longer than thirty minutes require much care and refinement if they are to be as uniformly successful as their shorter counterparts.[2] Occasionally, some persons can run to seventy-five minutes without having the element of time act as a barrier to their success. But this can rarely be accomplished by inflexible or insensitive speakers who are completely oblivious to the force of time. It can be accomplished only by those individuals who note that personal privilege and worth are revealed by their use or misuse of time.

Besides the element of time, the oral communicator must concern himself with the advantages and disadvantages of the *location*. The wise speaker realizes that certain subjects can be discussed in an elevator while others cannot; that certain topics "clash" with certain environments, others do not; that some subjects are definitely enlivened by certain environments. In making his judgments, the speaker must consider the general location (indoor, outdoor, home, office, school, church) as well as the specific location within those general areas. Is the front porch better suited for certain discussions than the living room of the home? Is the secretary's office more advantageous to some communicative endeavors than the private office of the employer? Is an outside room in a factory or hotel better suited for seminars than one located on an inner courtyard?

The speaker should also try to select an area suitable in *size* to his audience. Ideally, a location is "just large enough" to accommodate the needs of the activity. One does not choose to speak to a group of twenty-five persons in an auditorium which seats four hundred. Neither does he choose to teach thirty-five students in a room designed for fifteen. Less obviously, the efficient communicator also avoids engaging in communi-

---

2. Thomas R. Lewis and Ralph G. Nichols, *Speaking and Listening* (Dubuque, Iowa: Wm. C. Brown Company Publishers, 1965), p. 35.

cation (particularly on certain subjects) with one individual while twenty others are crowded around him.

Next, each communicator assumes responsibility for all *accessory* aspects of the location which may influence the outcome of his efforts. Such things as lighting, acoustics, heating, ventilation, and storage requirements may hamper or destroy rewarding communication. Two of the greatest barriers to communication are bad lighting and inadequate ventilation. Many studies conducted for industry have demonstrated the enervating effect on the average individual of insufficient, badly directed or surplus lighting. It is less important to have intensity illumination than to have light evenly distributed throughout an area. Whenever possible, lighting should be natural rather than artificial. Indoor locations must be adequate, also, in terms of ventilation if the speaker is to be successful. Hot stuffy, smoke-filled rooms are not conducive to energetic speakers or responsive listeners. But, then, neither are locations which permit the auditors to be exposed to cold, drafts, or alternating periods of discomfort.

Finally, the communicator must be cognizant of the various possibilities for *distractions*. Aside from the harmful effects of bad lighting and ventilation already mentioned and the easily imagined barriers imposed by poor acoustics, one must also know of the impediments created by ambient noise. Microphone feedback, whirring slide projectors, scraping chairs, and side conversations should be as great a concern as traffic noise, road repair machinery, or cafeteria sounds. Furthermore, the good communicator strives to remove or minimize those distractions which arise from poorly displayed models, improper and irrelevant slides, charts, maps, or uncovered windows opening onto a busy thoroughfare or a wonderful vista. These matters may seem trivial but because of them, listeners may be placed under great handicap.

Having exercised careful judgment in the matters of time, location, and freedom from distraction, the efficient communicator turns his attention to the more specific arrangements for listening. Seating arrangements for the listeners should go beyond the basic consideration of number. They should include a scrutiny of the comfort level (too much is more a detriment than not enough), traffic flow, need for identification (special groups or individuals), and other detailed requirements. More important, however, planning in the more formal situations should concentrate upon optimum order. Ideally, the participants in a communicative situation should be seated reasonably close together. Obviously enough allowance must be made for work needs and matters of comfort, but arrangements should eliminate empty chairs or empty rows between participants. Except for group discussions, listeners numbering fewer than twenty should be seated in a semicircular, triangular, or rectangular pattern. When there are more than twenty auditors, classroom or theatre style seems to offer fewer problems. The principal factor in the selection of seating arrangement (not predetermined by room size, special programs, etc.) is the opportunity for easy eye contact between listeners and speaker.

Speaking arrangements are another important facet of the oral communicator's total concern. The need for platforms or lecterns varies with the proficiency of the speaker, the nature of the audience, and the formality of the situation. Generally, larger audiences demand the presence of platforms, lecterns, and other such arrangements. If there is much use of graphic materials, slides, and other visual aids, a slightly elevated speaking platform is in order. In addition, a small table adjacent to the speaker's stand provides the speaker with a convenient working area, if one is necessary. It is the speaker, also, who must make the provisions for unusual audiovisual equipment, management, and movement of props, distribution of handout materials, and so forth. On the other hand, in less formal situations and with fewer auditors, the good communicator moves away from special equipment and endeavors to get closer to his listener. Elimination of such physical barriers tends to do just that.

SUMMARY

The oral communicator must give as much thought to maximizing or minimizing certain elements of the psychophysical environment as he does to the various arguments within his message. If he is sensitive to this need, he will attend to the matters of time (month, day, hour, as well as length and sequence of message), location (including such accessory considerations as lighting, ventilation, and acoustics), distractions, listening and speaking arrangements. As Hollingsworth asserted long ago:

> ". . . the 'atmosphere' of the meeting place is an important factor, and . . . is due to the joint effectiveness of two influences. One is found in the immediate physical or mechanical features of the premises; the other is found in the faint revival of feelings of the sort which members of the audience have . . . experienced in meeting places of each particular kind."[3]

PRACTICAL REMINDERS

Propositions
1. People listen more discriminately during morning hours.
2. Talks are less effective if more than forty-five minutes long.

---

3. H. L. Hollingsworth, *The Psychology of the Audience* (New York: American Book Company, 1935), p. 171.

Skills of the Speaker: Situation Analysis

3. Poor lighting and ventilation distract more than ambient noise.
4. Audience seating should be controlled by the speaker.
5. Listener response is affected by the physical site.

Exercises
1. Construct a checksheet designed to improve situation analysis.
2. How should a talk be altered when a physical site requires a standing audience?
3. What does the speaker do when listeners begin to fall asleep?

Readings

Brown, W. and Wong, H. "Effects of Surroundings Upon Mental Work," *Journal of Comparative Psychology*, August, 1923, pp. 319-326.

Fraisse, Paul. *The Psychology of Time*. New York: Harper & Row, Publishers, 1963.

Furbay, Albert L. "The Influence of Scattered versus Compact Seating on Audience Response." *Speech Monographs*, XXXII June, 1965, pp. 144-148.

Inman, W. S. "The Moon, the Seasons and Man." *British Journ. Med. Psychol.*, 24 (1951), 267ff.

Perkins, H. V. "Climate Influences Group Learning." *Journal of Educational Research*, October, 1951, pp. 115-119.

Schultz, Duane P. "Time, Awareness, and Order of Presentation in Opinion Change." *Journal of Applied Psychology*, August, 1963, pp. 280-283.

Winick, C., and Holt, H. "Seating Position as Nonverbal Communication in Group Analysis." *Psychiatry* 24 (1961), 171-182.

Chapter 6

SKILLS OF THE SPEAKER— DELIVERY

The speaker who has carefully conceived, organized, and developed his message according to the needs of his listeners can still fail in his communication by ignoring the problems of delivering the message. To minimize the barriers imposed by poor delivery, the serious speaker studies relevant aspects of rehearsal and presentation.

REHEARSAL

To experience proficiency in any human process, the individual must rehearse regularly, purposefully, systematically, and realistically. This is as true of the process of speaking effectively as it is of writing, finding a square root, or driving a car. The various acts which comprise a process must be carefully practiced until they are committed to the realm of habit. Again it must be remembered that mere experience does not provide a guarantee of efficient learning. In oral communication, particularly, if experience were the only ingredient necessary to proficiency, all normal adults would be effective speakers since they have had years of experience. The thousands of people enrolled in speech courses do not suffer from want of experience; rather, they suffer from the lack of scheduled, purposeful, and realistic experience. To become proficient as a communicator (in the more formal situations especially), the individual must allocate part of his total schedule to the matter of rehearsal.

For best results rehearsals should begin four or five days before the actual performance. Anything less would represent haste and result in inefficiency. These rehearsal periods can be used most effectively if the rehearsal procedures follow certain basic principles.

Principles of Rehearsal

In keeping with the admonitions of psychologists and educators,[1] the

1. See H. F. Spitzer, "Studies in Retention," *Journal of Educational Psychology* (1939), pp. 641-656.

Skills of the Speaker: Delivery

rehearsals recommended here reflect the characteristics of being *regular, purposeful, systematic,* and *realistic.*[2]

Regular experience (or training) in the form of rehearsals is the basic requirement for the acquisition of new habits. As applied to habits of effective presentations, the individual must plan on a number of distinct rehearsal periods. He must understand that five practice sessions spaced over a period of five days are infinitely superior to five practice periods crammed into a two-hour period. Moreover, he must understand that equality of action is also required. In rehearsing a talk, the speaker must repeat the same procedures or activities although, of course, always striving to perform them in better fashion. This is also true of rehearsals that result in major content or procedural changes. By the time the speaker has arrived at the practice stage, major changes should be avoided. If absolutely necessary, such changes should be restricted to the first few practice sessions so that the sessions closest to the actual performance will closely approximate the real thing. The principles of regularity, then, must apply to time and method of rehearsal.

Purposeful rehearsals are those which are undertaken with conscious effort. This is to say that mere mechanical drill is seldom of value for anything other than the simplest of mechanical habits. Unless the speaker is deliberately aware and appreciative of the significant aspects of speaking, he will not improve because the habits will not become fixed. What has been called "conscious awareness" might well be referred to as the ability to *experience and simultaneously witness the act of experiencing.* Retention is increased whenever the individual is aware of his act of experiencing and does something toward insuring the repetition of only the perfect actions or associations.

Systematic rehearsals are those which, in addition to being regular, demonstrate progressive order. In other words, instead of being exactly the same as the preceding session, each rehearsal period ought to be more advanced. Toward this end, the speaker should arrange his practice periods so that the closer he gets to the actual day of presentation, the more like the actual presentation his rehearsal will be. While the first sessions may include use of outlines, the last sessions ought to completely duplicate the final presentation.

Realistic rehearsals are patterned as closely as possible after the actual experience. Again, it must be remembered the individual learns best only that which he actually rehearses. Should a speaker rehearse a formal presentation by muttering to himself while riding to work on the bus, he will learn only to become proficient in muttering on the bus. The speaker should avoid continual interruptions, diverse practice situations, incom-

2. H. G. Rahskopf, *Basic Speech Improvement* (New York: Harper & Row, Publishers, 1966) pp. 30-32.

plete rehearsals, imperfect aids, and the like. He should strive to practice in physical and psychological atmosphere close to that of the actual presentation. If nothing more, this kind of realistic practice will furnish the poise that usually accompanies individuals operating in familiar surroundings. Moreover, the presentation is effective in proportion to the degree in which the practice periods duplicate the conditions of the actual presentation.[3]

Types

Rehearsals, of course, may be of various kinds. In this section, the concern will be with the merits of *individual* and *group practice* sessions. The ideal program for rehearsals makes allowances for the utilization of both types, with the former acting as the prerequisite for the latter.

During individual rehearsals, after the material for the presentation has been selected, arranged, and refined according to the demands produced by efficient audience and situation analysis, the speaker must strive to make the ideas more a part of him. In both individual and group practice sessions, this is accomplished by the regular, purposeful, systematic, and realistic rehearsals mentioned earlier. Nevertheless, familiarity with the material comes best during individual practice sessions where the speaker, without the distracting element of a listener, may feel free enough to read from an outline. This procedure helps to fix the sequence of ideas in mind by eliminating any errors introduced because of poor memory. The presence of an audience during initial practice sessions is often translated into a tendency to emphasize delivery rather than content. In individual sessions, the speaker must try to establish a close familiarity with the material and until this is achieved drop all other considerations.

The practice sessions ought to adhere closely to the principles of rehearsal stated above, adding the consideration of *recitation, repetition,* and *rhythm* to insure learning. In this regard, the speaker should deliver all versions of the talk aloud; to retain the good habits which can be gotten from feedback, he should practice by using audible recitation. This is extremely important. In addition to the benefits of improved articulation, volume, pausing and phrasing, pitch variation, and so forth, the speaker who practices aloud receives valuable aid in timing. Unless delivered in the vocal manner similar to that required by the actual performance, the speaker will not have a good idea of the time required to present the talk even though furnished with a well-planned outline.

Advantages also accompany the wide use of repetition. Rote learning is most helpful when one is seeking to fix mechanical and uncomplicated

---

3. See H. Woodrow, "The Effect of Types of Training upon Transference," *Journal of Educational Psychology* 18 (1927), pp. 159-172.

acts, but it is also of use in rehearsing oral presentations which are comprised of many dynamic and complex activities. The speaker who has rehearsed the main ideas of a presentation a minimum of five to seven times achieves a good degree of content familiarity. But it is essential that the speaker emphasize the ideas rather than the words during those practice sessions. With the exception of certain key phrases and sentences, care should be exercised to prohibit unnecessary word repetition between practice sessions. In this way, the speaker can learn to utter the same thought by using a variety of words and phrases. At the actual performance he will not be confronted by the inability to think of "the one word" which describes his thought; he can choose among three or four alternatives.

More ease in learning is added by rhythm. In the extreme example of the jingle or singing commercial, one sees something of this added ease in learning. In like manner, poetry which has marked rhyme and meter tends to be memorized more rapidly than material not having these qualities. In most oral discourse there is an inherent rhythm which can be accentuated during the process of learning to improve retention. With extra care, the practicing speaker can create a rhythm out of movement from *one idea to another, from main points to subsidiary points, from one mood to another, and from variations in vocal emphasis.* Characteristic phrasing and varied lengths of pausing also afford opportunities for effective rhythm. However it is accomplished, rhythm properly used will enable the speaker to learn his material with greater ease.

Finally, individual rehearsals might be made more profitable by the judicious use of a tape recorder. If utilized, the machine should be set up so that it requires no act of maintenance during the time of the rehearsal. That is, the speaker should not have to interrupt his practice to reverse reels or cassettes, rewind tape, or replace the microphone. The recording can act as a monitor to faithfully report errors in content and delivery which tend to slip by the speaker who attempts to listen to himself. Any corrections should be noted on the outline and note cards for subsequent rehearsals.

Although practice before a group appears to approximate most closely the conditions of the actual preformance, it can work against effective presentations. In the first place, practicing before a group can instill in the speaker certain habits or attitudes of unreality which might interfere with proper adjustment to the ultimate audience. It is possible for the speaker to become very good at *practicing* (rather than *giving*) talks before groups. In the second place, most group rehearsals or "dry runs" place an undue burden upon a practicing speaker. As they are often handled, these "group critiques" devolve into personal opinion forums with certain critics crystallizing all that is negative. Nevertheless, when properly administered, the group critique does offer the speaker the opportunity for a "shakedown" situation. The best views of many minds are unquestionably superior to one mind. And only in an audience situation can the speaker really test understanding. When properly administered, group critiques can and do offer much help to the conscientious speaker.

But rehearsals are only preparatory. The ultimate test is the talk itself, the actual communicative experience for which all previous preparation was made. Certain concerns which could not be sufficiently defined to be fully rehearsed become, in the final presentation, matters which must be understood and controlled. Among these are the use of *primary aids* (bodily action) and *supplementary aids* (audiovisual material).

PRESENTATION

Oral communication is an incomplete act without proper use of *bodily action*. Posture, gesture, movement, and voice remain the universal signs of speaking activity. Without them, speech would not exist; with them, speech is inextricably bound to man's basic nature. From the earliest times, man recognized the strength of this bond and sought to use it as an aid to his own progress. The primitive tribes of Asia, Africa, and Polynesia placed as much emphasis upon the "seen" communication as on the "heard." The Greek civilization before the advent of Christ taught its young that proper management of the body was a continuing and important part of their total development as citizens. During the Middle Ages and the Renaissance, special study was directed to bodily movements as they applied to communication. Giovanni Della Casa, important Renaissance literary figure who helped to establish the civilized behavior patterns of the Western world, offered the view that:

> Polite people ought therefore to be mindful of the need for restraint such as I have described in their manner of walking, standing, or sitting, and in all that they do, in their gestures and in their dress, when they speak and when they are silent . . . .[4]

One scholar found, as far back as the seventeenth century, that he could get closer to an understanding of his fellows if he composed his face and body parts to suit the habitual pattern of the people with whom he associated. In this way, he pioneered the thought that by adjusting the body to suit certain universal postures associated with love, anger, pain,

---

4. Giovanni Della Casa, *Galateo*, translated by R. S. Pine-Coffin (Baltimore, Md.: Penguin Books, Inc., 1958), pp. 94-95. Note also the advice in Thomas Elyot, *The Governor* (1531); John Bulwer, *Chirologia* and *Chironomia* (1644); Francis Bacon, *The Advancement of Learning*, IX, 2.

Skills of the Speaker: Delivery 99

and the like, these very feelings or emotions could be called forth.[5] The necessary corollary is that, in proportion as the body is prevented from assuming such universal postures or patterns, the feeling or emotion will not be felt.

In the twentieth century, while the thought expressed above may not have universal support, the oral communicator realizes that man is still influenced by the meaningful actions of the human body—whether his own or another's. It is this very realization which underlies the concept of *empathy*. As used by most modern scholars, empathy refers to the universal human tendency to become involved *in* the actions and thoughts of another. Crying as another cries, laughing as another laughs, feeling the tenseness we detect in another are all common manifestations of empathy at work. While this tendency is more prevalent among the younger members of society, it exists in all. And to the degree that it does exist in all social beings, the oral communicator has available to him another avenue through which he can effect a communion of ideas and feelings. In addition to the message delivered orally, the speaker has the opportunity to deliver it visually as well. Aware of the need to unite these audiovisual messages, the oral communicator works to improve his use of such primary aids as *posture, gesture,* and *movement*.

Posture, as noted in Chapter I, is among the significant nonverbal clues to inner tensions, feelings, and attitudes. Postures can be "friendly," "combative," "indifferent," "confused," and even "exalted." One who stands before another as though the weight of the world were on his shoulders will obviously issue forth a metamessage which differs substantially from one whose body is alert and responsive. While there is no one correct posture for all activities and for all persons, there is an optimum for each person in each activity. Thus, while a short, muscular person may find it convenient and helpful to stand with his weight distributed unevenly (more on one foot than on the other), a taller person doing the same thing will appear ungainly and will draw attention away from his oral message. To be efficient, posture must contribute rather than detract from the communicator's message. Posture which permits the speaker to be free from gesturing and movement without each time demanding dramatic adjustments is efficient.

Gesture, as with posture, is a basic part of the individual's personality since it is tied to early patterns of neuromuscular activity. The feeling is that although gestures may mislead the listener, they do so less often be-

---

5. Tommaso Campanella (1568-1639) was the obvious forerunner of the James-Lange theory of emotions.

cause they are more deeply associated with the real nature of the individual. Just as penmanship tends to reveal hidden aspects of personality, so gestures during the act of oral communication furnish significant clues to one's inner traits. In any given situation, one person may laugh, another may twitch, and another may cough. Because of Puritan etiquette and distorted emphasis on the use of gestures, most Anglo-Saxons have been taught to suppress or disguise their gestures. Such training has helped develop the "unconscious hypocrites" whose words and actions do not coincide. It has helped, also, in the maintenance of a paradoxical attitude in most listeners who have been taught that one can speak efficiently without gestures, but who continue to feel uneasy when forced to participate in prolonged "blind" communication. When they are prohibited from viewing the speaker with the necessary eye contact, the general reaction is to become less and less interested in the message.

Efficient gestures are those which are (1) suitable to the communicator, (2) not distracting, and (3) not sustained. Unfortunately, there exist today many persons who feel that "training in gestures" is the easiest and fastest way to improve as a communicator. Underlying this belief is the idea that all persons should be trained to make the same gestures in similar situations. If, as has already been discussed, gestures are usually an inherent aspect of an individual's personality, attempting to alter one's pattern of gestures may be an attempt to alter one's personality. While this is, at times, advisable, it should not become standard practice. The tall person is structurally suited to certain types of gestures and unsuited to others. The person raised in an environment which stressed careful and sensitive body movements would find it most unnatural and distressing to assume a pattern of flamboyant actions. As stated in Principle A,[6] effective speech is also selectively particular—this applies to gesture patterns of the speaker as well as to special demands of the listener and occasion.

On the other hand, if one's normal pattern of gestures includes certain aspects which are distracting, then they should be minimized or eliminated. Persons who have a habit of smiling indiscriminately, those who automatically "stab" their points home and always in the same way must work to eliminate or modify such gestures. It goes without saying that certain gestures which are distasteful and obviously unpleasant should be replaced as soon as possible. But simple things such as scratching one's head, ear, or nose, putting one's hand in a pocket, or wiping perspiration from one's brow need not be avoided unless they become habitual. A speaker who fights to suppress his tendency to do these things as he feels the need will inevitably add to his feeling of tension and thereby interfere with his own effectiveness.

6. See Chapter 2.

But even these simple and normal gestures, if sustained, can become distracting. A speaker who continually places and replaces his hands in his pockets will decrease his effectiveness as will one who continually scratches his nose or loosens his tie. In short, gestures of consequence are those which are familiar, transient, and spontaneous.

Equally important in the consideration of bodily gesture is the matter of eye contact. Long considered to be "the mirrors of the soul," the eyes provide most observers with information relative to the speaker's sincerity, goodwill and flexibility. Most listeners tend to eschew speakers who refuse to look at them. The feeling is generated that the communicator is "not to be trusted" or that he does not really "care for his immediate listeners." A simple experiment will serve to prove the point. If, with the very next person encountered, one would carry on a legitimate communication *while maintaining a fixed* stare at the listener's left shoulder, the nature of the interference mentioned would be made clear. Discriminate eye contact sends forth a feeling of care and concern for the immediate audience as opposed to a generalized and abstract responsibility revealed in memorized manuscript or "canned" speeches which encourage fixed or "glassy" eye behavior.

From a concern with these more limited types of bodily action, the wise oral communicator turns to a study of the role of movement in speech. As with posture and gesture, there exists no single pattern of movement applicable to all persons in all situations. Yet, many of the financially successful charm schools and private institutes train their students to adopt some such pattern. The alumni of such courses can be identified by their stereotyped activity ranging from three paces forward at the beginning of new points in their messages to one step sideward when presenting a new example. What both students and instructors fail to realize in such instances is that *patterns of any kind lose their effectiveness in proportion as they become standard or universal.* With movement, as with gesture, the conscientious communicator works to free himself of the belief that it is automatically to be avoided. He concentrates on recognizing his own patterns and moves to eliminate those which are distracting or sustaining. In the end, he recognizes that discriminate movement relaxes the listener and relieves the speaker of tensions generated by a static position.

To this point, the discussion has concentrated on the speaker's effective use of such primary aids as posture, gesture, and movement. A word must now be said about the remaining aid contained within the speaker: *voice*.

If physical movement is inherently tied to one's real personality, then his voice must be even more so since it depends on such physical activity. The human voice, it will be realized, can hardly be produced by an inert, totally paralyzed person. As the individual removes himself further and further from the complete state of paralysis to the ideal state of alertness, his voice becomes a true "sign of life." Without any training in the matter, most individuals use voice as an index to another's personality, as has been mentioned in Chapter 1. If one encounters a comely female carefully groomed and tastefully dressed, his first impressions would probably be favorable. But if, upon speaking, she revealed a harsh and metallic voice studded with misarticulations and obsolete pronunciations, those first impressions would tend to be replaced. Friendliness, aggressiveness, and general emotional stability are revealed by the quality, pitch, volume, and rate of one's voice. And, as with the more overt bodily action and as revealed by Principle C, modification of unpleasant or ineffective vocal qualities probably means a modification of the deeper personality factors underlying these qualities. But personality changes of this sort are not always necessary since indifference, fear, or lack of training often accounts for distorted and ineffective vocal qualities. In most cases, it is enough to have a strong desire to understand what is involved and to improve.

Aside from cases in which definite pathology is involved, the most fundamental requirement the oral communicator must meet regarding voice is its responsiveness, audibility, intelligibility, and pleasantness. It should be flexible and vital, easily heard and understood by the auditors, and free from unpleasant elements. In other words, the speaker's *quality, pitch, volume,* and *rate* must be coordinated in each act of oral communication if it is to be successful; to the degree that one or the other is warped, defective, or inappropriate, good communication is impaired.

The unique quality of one's voice is shaped by the structure and use of certain parts of the body. The size, shape, and lining of his resonating cavities and the nature of his bones and muscular system all help define the characteristic quality which in turn helps others identify him. If the resonating cavities are small and the bone structure is light, the quality (or tone, or timbre) will tend to be lighter and higher than if the opposite conditions prevail. Swollen lining (due to infections) and tense vocal muscles will produce more modifications. At the expense of oversimplification, it can be said that most problems of nasality. hoarseness, breathlessness, or uncertain voices can be aided immensely (if not solved completely) by more purposeful and discriminating use of the cavities and muscles involved in voice production. As people get older, there is a tendency to restrict the jaw movements associated with effective use of the resonating cavities. Continued and purposeful practice, as mentioned in the earlier section of this chapter, in exaggerated jaw, throat, and lip movements will help prevent the tendency from becoming a habit. Also, under certain psychological stresses, the human voice changes significantly. If this becomes habitual or even quite constant, the quality of the voice will become fixed as the muscles and organs find it increasingly easier to fall into these patterns of action. Hence, variety in mood and flexibility in use of vocal organs and muscles are the best insurance for a voice with a pleasant and effective quality.

Next to quality, the most recognized element of one's voice is pitch. Pitch involves the individual's ability (or lack of ability) to raise and lower his voice as compared with the established sounds of a musical scale. The good communicator evidences a range of at least one octave (eight notes) on the musical scale; the average communicator restricts his range to approximately four or five constant pitches and has a natural pitch located usually at one end or the other. Pitch changes are determined primarily by changes in the length and tension of the speaker's vocal folds and secondarily by the degree of tension throughout the rest of the muscular system. The most effective speakers are those who can control their vocal folds and reduce the amount of unnecessary tension throughout the rest of the body in order to utilize a great and continuous variety in pitch. It is through such variety, through the absence of a monotone, that the important inflections and modulations involved in clear meaning are produced. However, if such variety becomes constant, then the individual reveals a circumflex pattern of inflection (often attributed to immigrant Scandinavians when first learning English phonetics). As with a monotone (or absence of variety), the circumflex inflection (singsong) can be a deterrent to successful communication since it calls attention to itself. Suffice it to say at this point that, excepting serious cases stemming from physiological causes, pitch problems can be overcome by most individuals who communicate with Principles A, B, and C in mind.

Regardless of the idea or feeling, unless an auditor hears (or sees) it, there can be little influence exerted by it. To most people, oral symbols are much more than sounds. They are, in fact, a kind of physical contact. They can soothe, agitate, frighten. The whispering harmonious qualities of lullabies and the harsh, staccato, loud nature of most curse words indicate this phenomenon. Loud words, acting as aural gestures affect the adrenal glands, quicken the pulse, interrupt the breathing pattern, and so forth. For this reason, one's characteristic voice volume should reflect the same viability as in pitch. The strength needed for strong voices is dependent on proper control of the breath stream during the exhalation phase of respiration. This control, in turn, is affected by efficient use of the abdominal muscles, the diaphragm, the muscles of the chest, back, and throat. Increased tension in the abdominal muscles coupled with a relaxation of the diaphragm and selected muscles of the chest compress the lungs and force the breath stream against the vocal folds with enough force to increase the volume. Unless the oral communicator varies the volume of his voice in response to his intended meanings in a certain place, at a certain time and with certain listeners, the full effect of his message could easily be compromised.

The speaker's rate of speech, the number of words he speaks per minute, also carries an impact which may add or detract from the success of the communicative experience. A rate which is above the normal range of 150 to 185 words per minute will prove difficult to attend and inefficient in terms of goals achieved (unless one's purpose is to agitate, confuse, and unnerve another). On the other hand, speech which is below the normal rate can be equally irritating and confusing. Thus, as with most other aspects of the entire speaking process, the key ingredient in an efficient rate of speech is variety. At times, because of the nature of the listener or the subject or the occasion, a slower rate is even better than a normal one (when speaking over a public address system in a very large auditorium). At other times, a faster rate achieves the desired end sought by the speaker (when seeking to divert attention). Normally, the full range is used in rhythmical fashion.

Rhythm in speech reveals the true individuality of the speaker. How he moves from syllable to syllable (sensitively or indifferently), from word to word in casting his sentences, from thought to thought in forging his arguments, and from mood to mood in giving special meaning to the whole, encourages or discourages listener participation.

Audiovisual Material

Good speakers are also aware of the advantages and disadvantages of using *audiovisual material*. Aside from inadequate audience analysis, the most common error in more formal talks is the misuse of such material. The belief has grown that success is assured in proportion to the number of aids employed. The available evidence indicates that wise use of certain aids does help the speaker's cause. Those aids, properly designed and used, clarify meaning and increase understanding.

When properly designed, audiovisual material is *drawn from the message*. Aids prepared and used by other speakers for other occasions are to be shunned. To be effective, aids must be patently related to the message and the audience. Further, they should be constructed after the talk has been organized and only for those sections needing more clarity and emphasis.

When properly designed, aids are *suited to the occasion*. Assuming that material is to modify listener behavior, it should be constructed so it falls within the range of listener experience. Furthermore, it must be familiar to the speaker and appropriate to the time and place of the communication. Cartoons for adult audiences and tape recordings of poor quality, for instance, can rarely be defended.

When properly designed, aids are *technically adequate.* To improve the communion between speaker and listener, the audiovisual material must be heard and seen by the communicants. Too often, aids are made by artists inexperienced in oral communication and used by speakers who, insensitively and carelessly, judge the adequacy of an aid by their own ability to see or hear it. Aids should be tested in the actual physical setting in which they will be employed, or one similar to it.

When properly used, aids reflect care and concern for the *needs of the listener, the occasion, and the speaker.* This attitude is best demonstrated in the preparation and the presentation of the material. Regardless of form, the material should be brought into view only as it becomes a part of the immediate discussion. It must be covered or removed when not in use so distraction may be minimized. Also, all aids should be positioned beforehand to prevent needless waste of time during the presentation and to allow both speaker and listener to view them with minimal interruption of eye contact, unnatural changes in position, or other adjustments which undermine effective communication. Finally, the aids must be timed properly so they do not occupy more than thirty per cent of the total time of the talk.

Despite popular opinion to the contrary, no one aid is perfect. Good speakers retain a flexible and critical attitude toward all such material and realize that efficiency varies with speaker, listener, and occasion. Still, certain demonstrated advantages and disadvantages of the more popular forms ought to be known.

Among mechanical aids (those requiring mechanical equipment), movies have a high degree of popularity because they are easy to use, economical of time, and unique in format. Films allow for observation of matters generally unavailable to the naked eye—growth phenomenon, complex coordinations of color, sound, action, and so forth. Nevertheless, films can be disadvantageous when they dominate the communicative experience. For this reason, they must be carefully previewed so their relevance can be ascertained and highlighted. Unless the film is self-contained, the speaker should allow some time for discussion after its showing. Finally, the inflexible nature of time and content demand that the film be used as a unit or not at all.

Slides are not so inflexible. They are, moreover, easy to produce, use and adapt. They benefit the auditor by encouraging attention and increasing retention. They benefit the speaker by allowing him to use materials (maps, graphs, tables) which may be too large or too small in their original form. Furthermore, slides help the speaker by allowing him to unify attention and direct it to areas he feels are important. But caution must be used to prevent poor quality (too much text or color, too elementary) and poor quantity (too much). An effective rule is one slide (if needed) for every five minutes of presentation, shown as needed rather than as part of a block before or after the talk.

Projections (opaque or transparent) are even more flexible. With these, the speaker is free to use a more spontaneous approach; maps, charts, and pictures found in available texts can be used in their regular forms without the special expenditure of time, money, or effort. Transparencies permit, in any sequence desired, the construction of charts and diagrams as the speaker progresses. Moreover, he can use projections without breaking eye contact with his audience if he is careful in selecting the number, frequency, and kind to be used. In particular, he should avoid using typewritten transparencies since they are too light, too uniform, and too familiar to impress most people.

Recordings have gained wide support within the last decade because more material is available and what is available is easily usable and adaptable and is dramatic in effect. With careful use, the wise speaker can strengthen his effort by creating certain moods and by using the thoughts and voices of authorities respected and admired by the listeners. But as with other aids, recordings must be used in accordance with the general rules noted. They must also be previewed, introduced, and concluded by the speaker and tested under the same amplification as required during the final talk. Finally, in the event of mechanical failure, the speaker should be prepared to use the contents in the form of quoted material.

Aside from the mechanical aids, certain display material should be considered in any discussion of audiovisual aids. Like mechanical aids, displays must be used wisely. The size, form, color, number, and placement of labels, the progression of text, and so forth, must be carefully controlled by the speaker.

Maps, as a sample of this material, have as their chief function the graphic representation of distance, direction, location, size, and the like. The use of maps as supplements to oral communication is strengthened with the use of overlays and three dimensional forms, but weakened by excessive size, color, and detail.

Charts are used in order to highlight simple relations and total impressions and are proven most effective when they demonstrate simplicity and clarity. The "strip tease" chart by providing for an item by item revelation carries the greatest impact since it incorporates the unfolding feature mentioned in Chapter 1.

Graphs are best employed to represent statistical interpretations. Line graphs are best for indicating trends; bar graphs for quantitative relations; pie graphs for proportional relationships. In each instance, discreet cartoons and pictures can be used to highlight the relationships shown.

Writing boards, quite popular in industry and education, include such things as flannel and magnetic boards, flip charts and blackboards. Sim-

Skills of the Speaker: Delivery

plicity is the great strength and an indispensable requirement. These props also take advantage of the "unfolding" phenomenon since information can be revealed bit by bit as the speaker progresses. Important also is the flexibility which permits the visualization of concepts developed or developing in the immediate situation—if the speaker avoids crowding, poor handwriting, excessive speed, incomplete diagrams, and so forth.

Models (including dioramas) permit the display of items and relationships which are too large, too small, or too complex to be placed on one dimensional material such as slides and transparencies. Working models, of course, have the added advantage of movement but must be *used only as an aid* and not for *matters of interest*.

A complete understanding of audiovisual material used as aids in the communicative process can only be touched on in this book It should be remembered though that the aids are only as good as the care and concern shown in their planning and use.

SUMMARY

While practice does not make perfect, a regular, purposeful, systematic, and realistic rehearsal pattern will improve any person's ability as a speaker. One may practice by himself or in the presence of a carefully selected group. In either condition, one must apply recitation, repetition, and rhythm.

Bodily actions can help or hinder his communicative endeavors. His posture, gesture, and movement aid him and the listener when they are properly executed. In like manner, the efficient speaker may wisely use various supplementary aids in the audiovisual field. If these aids are directly related to the message, suited to the occasion, technically adequate and properly employed, they can furnish significant assistance. Mechanical aids (movies, slides, projections, recordings) as well as display aids (maps, charts, diagrams, boards, models) have certain advantages and disadvantages which the speaker should know. The basic philosophy governing the use of audiovisual material is that if lost after they have been constructed, the speaker should be able to continue his talk without them.

PRACTICAL REMINDERS

Propositions

1. Only perfect practice makes perfect.
2. Group rehearsals are best after private ones.
3. Posture, gesture, and movement must suit the speaker's personality and subject and the occasion.

4. Eye contact is a help in communicating with strangers or friends.//
5. Good speakers manifest rhythm and variety in their voices.
6. Properly designed and used, audiovisual material provides the speaker's communicative efforts with strength, color, and depth.

Exercises

1. Try to conduct daily activities without the spoken word. What areas offer the most difficulty? Which are least affected?
2. Go through the actions involved in shooting a pistol, a rifle, a bow and arrow, and a slingshot. Practice for ease and clarity of action.
3. Without voice, describe a blood relationship (brother, sister), a need for a fifty dollar loan, a preference for hot dogs or eggs.
4. Repeat precisely and rapidly: Lester likes lemons lovelier while Peter prefers peppers peeled; tan cotton candy clean cold combs.

Readings

Davitz, J. R., ed. *The Communication of Emotional Meaning.* New York: McGraw-Hill Book Company, 1964.

Fromm, Eric. *The Forgotten Language.* New York: Henry Holt & Company, Inc., 1951.

Geldard, F. A. "Some Neglected Possibilities of Communication." *Science* 131 (1960), 1583-1588.

Hall, E. T. *The Silent Language.* New York: Fawcett World Library: Crest, Gold Metal & Premier Books, 1959.

Mehrabian, A. "Communication Length as an Index of Communicator Attitude." *Psychol. Rep.,* 17 (1965), 519-522.

Scheflin, A. E. "The Significance of Posture in Communication Systems." *Psychiatry* 27 (1964), 316-331.

PART III

ORAL COMMUNICATION
Action and Reaction

We Listen Through a Screen
of Personal Experience

"A Photographer Looks at Himself,"
Vytas Valaitas, Photographer

Photography Annual, 1960.
Used by permission.

Chapter 7

SKILLS OF THE LISTENER—PREPARATION

UNDERSTANDING THE NATURE OF LISTENING

Effective listening is an activity which presupposes a precise degree of coordination in a sensory system which can receive aural symbols and an intellect which moves from symbol to message. Indeed, it is a manifestation of an even more profound coordination between two complex human beings—a purposeful, controlled, and alternating silence. Silence usually acts as the leveling agent, the common denominator in a communicative situation, and must be broken to establish individuality or true communion. In purposefully and systematically breaking silence, the communicants cooperate in creating social beings out of individual entities. In miraculous fashion, they each contribute toward directing the nature, scope, and speed of "unfolding" their intimate selves, their interiorities. As Balzac observed in his youth, the listening experience creates an opportunity for a true communion.[1]

Listening is as important to the human personality as protein is to the human body. In the absence of this ability—as a result of either physical or psychological deficiencies—the human personality develops in a warped fashion. The inability to participate in the act of communication usually results in isolation, confusion, frustration, and eventually madness. One can best see such responses in unfortunates who have been deafened by injury or disease, in the eyes of those who have been thrust into the middle of a conversation pursued in a foreign language, or in the activity of persons afflicted by the distorted and unintelligible sounds resulting from aphasia. Fortunately, advances in both research and training have brought the knowledge necessary to repair and develop the physical as well as the psychological aspects of listening. Man's current understanding of the process of listening goes far beyond the views published ten or fifteen years

---

1. Justin O'Brien, "Observer of the Human Comedy," *The Saturday Review* (July 9, 1966), p. 27.

ago. Whereas he once was concerned exclusively with the physical aspect (hearing), he is now aware of the equally important psycholinguistic phase; whereas once his focus was in assuring the clean and accurate perception of sound, his attention has progressed to the meaning drawn from that sound; whereas earlier concerns of education included training in the production and identification of the oral sounds of language, current views focus on increasing the nature and scope of experiences in order to increase understanding.

Most significant, however, new research in dissecting the listening experience has revealed it as a complex, complicated, mercurial, but teachable adventure. Those who strive to improve their listening proficiencies now begin with the realization that the enduring and perennial problem is to keep various aspects of the experience separated (recording, interpreting, evaluating), to keep divisions of thought distinct and comprehensible while moving from one to another, and to keep one's attention on main ideas instead of on the similar and related ideas which cluster about it and have no other effect than to weaken or confuse it. Sensitive listeners learn that the fluidity, flexibility, and adaptability of oral communication serve to strengthen and weaken, help and hinder, efficient listening.

Whatever their specialized emphasis, researchers and educators have been quite definite in underscoring the importance of effective listening in all phases of modern living. Most obviously, listening contributes to much, if not most, of our knowledge of our surroundings. Less obviously, listening offers a ready, universal, and effective means of contributing to the social process of civilization. By enabling others to define their doubts, outline their confusions, register their protests, test their judgments, and experiment with their dreams, the good listener furnishes the important catalytic force in the development of his fellows.

As with all phases of human activity, the trained individual is much more proficient than the untrained. Nuances are observed, precise coordination effected, and general economy of effort revealed by the actions of the trained individual in everything from combat to communication, from letter writing to listening.

The trained listener is one who understands that effective listening in a communicative situation *is an active response to audiovisual phenomena which are employed in a dynamic environment for the purpose of modifying human behavior.* An analysis of the foregoing definition will reveal many of the subtleties which escape the untrained listener. Most persons who have learned their listening habits by osmosis assume that listening is a passive process, that listening can be improved by reading, and that the listener is required only to be physically present, awake, and reasonably attentive. In truth, effective listening demands an active auditor who is either taking notes, asking questions, or contributing in some audiovisual way to the creative efforts of the speaker. It is in this way that the listener exercises his responsibility as a social organism by cooperating in the difficult task of maintaining a complex and dynamic relationship between subjective revelation and objective adjustment. With the cooperation of effective listeners, the speaker is able to measure his balance between the vertical axis (subjective concerns with self or between self and the Diety) and the horizontal axis (objective concerns with others) in his oral communication.

Effective listeners realize also that the process of oral communication is never restricted to forming, transmitting, and receiving the oral symbols of language. They are aware of the less obvious but equally important super- and substructures which attend the more obvious symbols used in ordinary communicative situations; they are aware of the metamessages discussed earlier. At times, for example, words actually are made to transcend themselves so they represent social gestures instead of personal conclusions. Such "extra structures" include the physical movements, or lack of movements, of the speaker (and to the sensitive speaker these same conditions in the listener), the time and place of the communication, the vocal reflections, the organization of the message, and many more. Moreover, the well-trained listener is constantly aware of the dynamics of time, mood, and various interactions of human personalities. He knows, as has been shown, that any communication delivered after lunch or late in the afternoon or just before dinner must be received with special care since his conditions of fatigue and distraction are greater at these times; that changing moods in the speaker must be reflected by greater flexibility in the listener. The obvious example of this kind of listening awareness is that shown by most good psychiatrists. But these same subtle appreciations are an important part of the listening habits of a good minister, doctor, teacher, or friend.

Only the most naïve individual would expect to exercise the same listening habits in both a formal lecture situation and an informal tête-a-tête with a girl friend. As pointed out previously, in each situation the over purpose, the allotted time, the status factors (teacher-pupil vs. friend-friend) and the like all operate to demand various degrees and kinds of involvement. In some cases, his involvement is restricted to a silent recreation of the images and feelings of the speaker; in some, he must urge or goad or evaluate by overt movements and audible questions; in others, he is directly and continuously involved by way of measured responses to the speaker's commands or requests. However, despite these variations, in each instance the dynamics of the communicative situation insure that *active involvement* will be the *sine qua non* of the effective listener (Principle B).

Finally, the best listeners realize that they represent the ultimate end for which each communication is designed. Good speakers keep this constantly in mind so necessary modifications can be made during the communicative act to insure the desired listener response. Good listeners, operating with this realization, exercise their responsibility for constant and continuing participation in creating, developing, modifying, and evaluating the communication by establishing a purpose for every listening experience. To conserve energy and insure a successful experience, effective listeners begin their listening activities by deciding if the purpose of the experience is *entertainment, information,* or *evaluation*. Few things are ever offered in communicative situations for no purpose at all. The purpose may be insignificant, hidden temporarily from both speaker and listener, simple or complex, but is inevitably present and serving as a directing force for both speaker and listener. Unless the auditor clearly defines his purpose and seeks to relate it to that of the speaker, he may gather confusion in the place of understanding. Many auditors have spent untold hours of time in abject disappointment and confusion only because they came prepared to be inspired while the speaker came prepared to furnish information. Professors, lecturers, doctors, lawyers, parents, and friends have often been charged with negligence, incompetence, and insincerity because the listeners expected one thing and were offered another.

One who determines that he enters into a specific communicative situation for the purpose of entertainment will not have to prepare in advance. When the pleasant passage of time is the only goal, the auditor involvement is variable in degree as well as continuity and he may laugh at a joke, talk to his neighbor in the middle of the next joke, daydream, and so on. In a word, his responsibilities are more personal although his social obligations never disappear.

On the other hand, when the effective listener determines his goal to be that of gaining information (facts, opinions, or interpretations), something more is required. Here, again, involvement is necessary to insure the success of the communicative experience but it is deeper and more extended than that required by the purpose discussed earlier. In addition to the adjustments which will be described shortly, the auditor who listens to gain information *must restrict his desire to evaluate the information in the process of gathering it.* The main objective is to record, not to criticize. What the speaker says is the most important phase of the initial communicative encounter since the listener's reaction—acceptance, rejection, interpretation, modification—is governed by it. Consequently, accuracy in

Skills of the Listener: Preparation

recording emerges as the desired goal of the effective listener in an information-gathering situation.

Finally, one may listen for evaluation. Sometimes the situation is such that the processes of gathering information and evaluation are practically simultaneous. Time or circumstance do not permit the distinct separation of these activities and, more often than not, error and misunderstanding result.[2] Unless they are separated, the average listener finds himself arguing with the first part of the speaker's statement while the speaker is offering another part to modify the first. In this way, arguments and decisions are based more on what the listener imagined than on what was actually said.[3] Proper evaluation follows information-gathering and does not begin until all the information is in and understood. Thus, prior to a final evaluation, the effective listener asks (1) What did the speaker say? (2) What did he mean? (3) What is his degree of competence in the subject? (4) What is the nature and degree of his prejudice toward the subject?

ADJUSTING TO THE DEMANDS OF LISTENING

Having decided upon his specific purpose, the listener must now turn to the task of assuring maximum benefit from his listening experience by adjusting to the physical and psychological environments in which his experience takes place.

While it is primarily the speaker's responsibility to select and maintain suitable physical surroundings for his communication, the listener must share his responsibility by overcoming certain minor disadvantages. Among these is the matter of physical placement; that is, the listener must choose a position (standing or sitting) which allows him to see and hear the speaker with a minimum of strain. It is not enough to assume that as long as one can hear the speaker he is suitably placed in terms of his listening responsibilities. A moment's reflection will call to mind the myriad instances where a speaker's mannerism defined the sub- or superstructure of his meaning and prevented a false or misleading interpretation by the auditor. More than this, of course, eye contact serves as an aid for the speaker. Unless the sensitive speaker has the advantage of noting the facial expressions, bodily postures or other physical activity engaged in by the active listener, he is unable to monitor his ideas or the manner of their delivery.

Proper physical placement also includes a concern for adequate light, heat, and ventilation. The stuffy, smoke-filled, dimly-lighted room is not conducive to effective listening except possibly for the purpose of enter-

2. Rogers, *op. cit.* pp. 14-15.
3. *Ibid.*, p. 15.

tainment. Many studies by industrial organizations have demonstrated the unquestioned deleterious effect of insufficient, badly directed or—oddly enough—surplus lighting on the average person. In like manner, ambient noise drains attention and energy much more than commonly realized. It is more important to effective listening to have a constant, even distribution of noise and light than to have an irregular, inconsistent attempt to control either one. Erratic microphone amplification, outside traffic noise, kitchen noises, and the like, if not taken care of by the speaker, must be adjusted to by the listener moving to a more advantageous position.

Another physical consideration, frequently overlooked, is the matter of time. Having a choice in the matter, the average listener ought to avoid important listening experiences which are presented during meal hours and in the late afternoon or evening. During these periods, the human body is besieged by internal stimuli which help to prevent or minimize listening effectiveness. Fatigue, unless dissipated by activity or replaced by nourishment, will interfere with sensation, perception, and judgment. Most people, during such moments, tend to become irritable and easily distracted. This is also the case when auditors are required to attend presentations which are longer than forty-five or fifty minutes. If the speaker does not provide momentary diversion through controlled questioning, relevant humor or some other type of audience response, the individual auditor should provide for it himself. This can be done, most easily, by shifting bodily postures, increasing or decreasing note-taking, asking a question of the speaker, and so forth.

Finally, the careful auditor gives due consideration to his physical comfort as defined by his seating or standing arrangements. Obviously, too much discomfort will interfere with his concentration and, hence, ought to be avoided or reduced. On the other hand, believing that one ought to be as comfortable as possible is a serious mistake. Too much comfort discourages the motivation necessary for successful listening. In the vernacular it may be said that "if you ain't hurting, you ain't pushing." This applies to effective listening as it does to any other successful endeavor of life. Complacency has never been the hallmark of successful societies, institutions, or individuals.

Aside from being adequately adjusted to the physical environment, it is necessary to emphasize adjustment to the psychological environment as well. Here, of course, the successful earwitness manifests continuing control of his emotional state. Personal problems are set aside (as much as possible) and full attention is directed toward what is being said. As mentioned earlier, the auditor should try to divorce *what* is being said from *who* is saying it until he has gathered *all of what is being said*. Often, all too often, misunderstandings are encouraged and maintained by the

Skills of the Listener: Preparation

habit of half-listening *or* nonlistening. Evaluations are made on the basis of the speaker rather than the idea, in terms of a party instead of a principle, or in consideration of status instead of sense. While it is difficult to withhold such judgments, while it is more the rule than the exception to reject what the speaker is saying even before he has completed his thought, the successful listener does precisely this. And this he does because he is aware of the "unfolding" aspect of communication talked about earlier; he is conscious of the link by link development of ideas, desires, and moods and, more often than not, of the listener's understanding of these phenomena; he is aware of his limitations which derive from his poor memory and his susceptibility for distraction.

SUMMARY

As it has been developed in this chapter, listening represents a human phenomenon which has physical and psychological aspects, individual and social consequences. It is an active response to audiovisual phenomena which are employed in a dynamic environment for the purpose of modifying human behavior. To engage in the activity with any measure of success, the sensitive listener strives to establish a purpose for each listening experience and then arranges his physical and psychological environments to contribute to a rewarding occasion.

PRACTICAL REMINDERS

Propositions
1. The responsibilities of speech are shared by the listener.
2. Most people are handicapped by poor listening habits.
3. Listeners react to speaker, message, and occasion.
4. Active involvement is indispensable to successful listening.
5. Too much comfort hinders rather than helps the sincere listener.

Exercises
1. Arrange with some friends to have a speaker (a) deliver a short talk blindfolded or (b) speak to an audience facing away from him. Record the reactions which relate to the contents of this chapter.
2. During a class exercise (with the instructor's permission) respond to a classmate's talk by frowning, grimacing, shrugging, etc. When he is through, ask his reaction to this.
3. Arrange for someone to ring a bell (or give some other clear signal) five or six times during another's talk. At the signal, class members should

record a "yes" or "no" to note whether they listened to the *idea being expressed at precisely that moment.* Total up the number of responses on either side to find out how attentive the class was.

READINGS

AMATO, P., and OSTERMEIER, T. "The Effect of Audience Feedback on the Beginning Public Speaker." *Speech Teacher,* 16 (1967), 56-60.

BRUNER, J. "On Perceptual Readiness." *Psychological Review,* 64 (1957), 123-152.

KELLER, P. "Major Findings in Listening in the Past 10 Years." *Journal of Communication,* 10 (1960), 29-38.

NICHOLS, RALPH G., and STEVENS, LEONARD A. *Are You Listening?* New York: McGraw-Hill Book Company, 1957.

ROGERS, CARL. "Communication: Its Blocking and Its Facilitation." *Northwestern University Information* 20:9-15, April 21, 1952.

Chapter 8

SKILLS OF THE LISTENER— PARTICIPATION

EFFECTING AN ACTIVE ROLE

At a time when man was developing his individual identity, when he was beginning to transport himself and his ideas with greater ease and frequency, and when he turned his attention to founding universities, there arose a slogan: *Mors et vita in manibus lingua* or "Life and death rest in the hands of the tongue." The saying was, at once, descriptive and prescriptive; it told what society had observed to be a fact while at the same time it offered instruction to all sensitive and intelligent persons. It called attention to the fact that human speech may act as a sword, a shield, or a lily. But more than this, while it urged for care in transforming experience into ideas and ideas into oral symbols because of their possible impact on another human being, *it presumed an auditor active enough to be affected.* To become misdirected, misshaped, or otherwise harmed by the oral symbols directed at him by another human, the listener must perceive, translate, and understand those symbols. What is not heard cannot be interpreted; what is not interpreted and applied can have only minimal impact upon the intelligent human being. At the base of every act of oral communication is the active listener (oneself or others) without whom the act of communication would be only a useless noise.

Listener activity may take many forms, but the most significant are those which involve recording and evaluation. As noted earlier, the natural tendency is to telescope these functions so they occur simultaneously. While this practice is the most common, it is far from the most efficient or the most rewarding. While this practice may be demanded, occasionally, by time, place, or circumstance, it should be avoided whenever possible. Each aspect of listening should be given distinct attention since it involves distinct and complicated demands from the listener.

Whether done mentally or in written form, the process of recording should be accompanied by definite and overt activity on the part of the listener. At the low end of the scale in regard to probable influence on listener learning are facial expressions, shoulder shrugs, smiles, laughs, nods, applause, and the like. These indications of involvement are an aid to the speaker since they estimate his effectiveness. To the listener, such activities serve as reinforcements to interest as well as memory. It is as though he were "swept up in the general stream of movement, intellectually and physically. . . ."[1] To both, such active involvement furnishes a bridge, a bond, a link, a force whereby the socialization of individuals is carried forth.

The first requirement of recording what was said is the *structuralization* of the presentation. In most oral communication there tends to be more chaff than wheat, more support than thesis. The effective listener strives to grasp the central idea, leaving subordinate materials unattended except in instances where the main idea is not understood or is unacceptable. He does not become involved in details and is not distracted by examples, statistics, stories, and the like. Moreover, he controls his tendency to embark upon tangential thoughts because he knows his task is to separate the main point from the mass of related though corollary ideas which can confuse and minimize. He reminds himself that, in proportion as the examples and illuminating details multiply, the initial thought grows fainter. He reminds himself, also, that he shares the human fault of poor and faulty observation.

Effective speakers consciously set the main ideas apart from their related thoughts by *pauses, increases* or *decreases in volume,* or by *clear transitions.* Even poor speakers are inclined to pause slightly before and/or after stating what they believe to be their major points. On occasion, they might even combine that pause with a volume change to call the listener's attention to the idea. Both good and bad speakers make use of transitions—the linguistic signposts designed to inform the listener of turns, depressions, retreats, and other variations in the stream of human reflection being presented by the speaker. The auditor who hears "the most important thing to remember . . ." hurries to record it *whether he thinks it important or not*. After noting this (verbatim if possible) he allows himself a moment of relaxation when he hears such expressions as "for example," "for instance," or "such as."

Thus, properly executed, the listener's record of the speaker's presentation manifests itself in outline form with only as many details necessary to provide him with an opportunity for reinterpretation or a final evaluation of a questionable thesis. No efficient listener (save the court reporters, stenographers, and other specialists paid to do otherwise), attempts

---

1. Dominic A. LaRusso, "Visible Communication: Bodily Action," in H. G. Rahskopf, ed., *Basic Speech Improvement* (New York: Harper & Row, Publishers, 1965), p. 219.

Skills of the Listener: Participation

to secure a written or mental record of the entire talk. Not only is it impossible, it is completely ridiculous to assume that it is necessary to the success of the more common instances of oral communication. The most urgent consideration is a record of the major parts of what was said rather than what the listener thought was said, a record of the symbols shaped and presented by the speaker rather than those synonyms and substitute phrases provided by the listener.

If the sensitive auditor is moved to make a pertinent observation regarding corollary thoughts, contradictions, insincerities, and the like, such short notations should be made in the margin of the notepad and put in parentheses or square brackets. Instantaneous impressions of the speaker's feelings, attitudes, pertinent items on his training and background which may be revealed during the presentation should all be recorded concisely and identified as observations by the use of brackets or some other similar device. In this way, what was said is kept separate from bits of information which may be used later in the process of evaluation.

Although related to the process of recording, the *art of questioning* is also a part of evaluation. However it is categorized, it is prominent enough to warrant a separate discussion. And any discussion of this basic aspect of man's intellectual pattern must include the obvious and traditional information regarding its use through the years.

Although indirectly a part of all traditions and a prominent part of the Biblical episodes, the art of questioning was given its greatest impetus by the antics of Socrates during the high point of Grecian civilization. In quest of his version of truth, Socrates felt the question to be more important than the answer since it served to define, direct, and color the answer. He reasoned that asking such a simple question as, "Do you believe in God?" prescribed his companion's thought. Nothing could be said of sport, economy, politics, or any other thing which the respondent preferred to think about at that moment. Further, Socrates thought it important to forge a process which minimized man's effort and maximized his reward by controlling his tendency to become involved in tangents. Accordingly, his practice focused upon shaping a specific question, gathering a response and from that response shaping a new question and, in turn, gathering a new response. His questions were always leading, based on concrete data, dependent on definitions and precise categories and, inevitably, moved from the known experiences of the respondent to the unknown. In this careful way, link by link, a literal chain of oral communication was formed.

Other great thinkers and teachers who followed Socrates, from Jesus to Mark Hopkins, placed a great deal of emphasis on properly-phrased, carefully-timed and sensitively-delivered questions. Any sensitive human and all successful listeners and speakers make the art of questioning a regular and continuing part of their communicative experiences. To do so, they operate with an understanding of the value, type, and use of good queries.

As the name implies, the question starts both the speaker and the listener on a quest or a search for something which is not already a part of their immediate environment. This something could be a feeling, an attitude, an understanding, or a bit of information which speaker and listener value enough to devote time and effort for its revelation. In itself, the question reveals an appreciation of another person—at least to the extent of realizing his presence. More than this, however, even the most trivial question reflects a degree of respect for another, a healthy lack of self-centeredness. Finally, the astute listener-speaker is cognizant of the indispensable role of the question in guiding thought, encouraging action, and controlling the normal unfolding phenomenon of life.

But efficient use must also include an understanding of the various kinds of questions which may be fashioned. In the broader aspects, there are questions of fact, interpretation, and value. Too often, the inept listener asks a question of fact, expects an interpretation in return, and, when it is not received, becomes confused or incensed. More often, however, questions of value are asked under the guise of fact or interpretation, thereby increasing the opportunities for misunderstanding. As with the need for separating record taking from evaluation, the careful listener is aware of the need for divorcing questions of fact from those of interpretation and value. More important, still, the listener should not accept an interpretative answer for a question of fact or value. If one is offered, he should persist in gathering the answer he needs.

Within each of these broad areas—fact, interpretation, value—the listener must still choose among several forms of questions. He may, for example, ask open or closed questions. The former permits an extended answer as in the case where one is asked, "What is your opinion of Harry Truman?" The respondent is prevented, by the very nature of the question, from answering "Yes" or "No." On the other hand, the questioner may feel the necessity of asking a closed question such as, "Do you think Harry Truman was a good president?" While he may extend his answer, the implicit invitation is for a simple and direct response. In the course of a multisided communication involving several people, the listener may see the need for directing his question more carefully to a named individual. He may ask, "Dr. Miller, is it your thought that mercy killing is unethical?" In this instance, since the respondent was alerted first, he may be saved from possible confusion and embarrassment due to a momentary wandering of the mind. If the question was phrased, "Is it your thought that mercy kill-

Skills of the Listener: Participation

ing is unethical, Dr. Miller?" the respondent may have to ask that the question be repeated. While other categories of questions may also be defined, the open, closed, and name questions represent the most basic types and are sufficient for this discussion.

As with other things, a knowledge and appreciation of value and types are but the prelude to use. Proper use of questions is predicated upon four basic rules:

1. Make certain of the respondent's attention prior to delivering the question.
2. Keep the questions *short, clear, simple,* and *definite.*
3. Be satisfied only with direct, relevant, and complete answers (although you may deem it necessary to accept others).
4. Whenever time and circumstance permit, develop a progression of thought via a series of interrelated queries.

Fairly secure in the knowledge of what was said as a result of his active note-taking and/or questioning, the concerned listener moves now to the process of evaluation.

When Professor Carl Rogers observed ". . . our research and experience to date would make it appear that breakdowns in communication, and the evaluative tendency which is the major barrier to communication, can be avoided," he was obviously underscoring the need for proper and timely evaluation.[2] Such an evaluation would begin with the message itself. It is at this point that the listener endeavors to go beyond what the speaker said by drawing upon his own training, experience, and research to prove or disprove, to accept or reject. Having heard what the speaker said and having determined by reflection on the main points that he understands what he meant, the listener must next apply some of the simple tests of logic alluded to in Chapter 4.

Logic, as logic, is an intricate and involved discipline which involves much time and study. As a basis for successful evaluation of various oral communications, it can be greatly simplified without impairing its value. In the first instance, since logic always involves a leap from one idea to another, the acceptability of the main point must be established; one must examine the idea from which the leap is made. This can be done, in simplest fashion, by trying to discover valid exceptions to that proposition. To the thought that "elementary level teachers are underpaid," the average listener can attach innumerable instances of incompetent teachers he has known who have drawn too much from public funds. By the same token, he can probably cite three or four teachers who make as much as professionals in other areas but work on a contract totaling 185 days. These ex-

2. Rogers, *op. cit.,* p. 9.

ceptions serve not so much to argue for the rejection of the proposition as to call for caution in concluding that "we need federal aid to education." Perhaps federal aid is needed, but it should be based upon something more than the broad and questionable statement that "elementary level teachers are underpaid." On the other hand, the statement "we had a Puerto Rican gardener once so I don't think we should vote for the Puerto Rican candidate for Senator," is best tested (again by collecting exceptions) by demanding a broader base for the conclusion. The old adage that "one raindrop does not constitute a storm" should be applied to any attempt to make a category or class or general statement from one example. The second step should be to examine the idea to which the leap is made and in the same manner described above.

In addition to testing the idea *from* and *to* which the logical leap is attempted, the listener must probe the relationship between them to determine if it is what the speaker describes it to be. He must ask, for example, if the connection between the two main ideas is clear, direct, and necessary. Can the transitional bridge between the major points be altered with as little or as much rationale as is used to maintain it? Can one change the statement "handicapped persons succeed *in spite* of their handicaps" with as much or as little substantiation as offered in presenting the first version? If so, then another reason for delaying the acceptance or rejection of the major propositions comes to the surface. By attending to the *function of the transition* used to connect the main points, the astute listener can also evaluate the acceptability of the speaker's logic. The speaker may feel that "John Smith is a poor teacher because he is from the East," but the efficient listener will take this as a conclusion which demands explanation. While each of the major ideas ("John is a poor teacher and he is from the East") may be true, one can hardly be connected with the other in a cause and effect relationship without explanation.

Quite obviously, the analysis of the oral message for logical soundness can be much more involved and protracted than the brief pattern discussed here. Specific and detailed questions are available which can be applied to syllogisms, statistics, analogies, and the like in the endeavor to evaluate arguments. However, in the heat, fluidity, and immediacy of most instances of oral communication, the average listener finds neither the memory nor the time nor the inclination to apply such extended tests to messages presented for his benefit. Nevertheless, in order to protect himself and exercise his responsibility to society, he should strive to apply some sort of analytic pattern to whatever he hears whenever he hears it.

Still, this is not enough. In the previous chapter, attention was called to a fact recognized by all successful auditors: in addition to the message itself, meaning is derived from certain nonmessage factors. These nonmessage factors have been spoken of before as constituting sub- or superstructures which accompany the oral symbols used. They include physical movements of the speaker, tone of voice, selection of time and place for the communication, and the like. These sub- or superstructures, in effect, produce a metamessage; these added ingredients very often combine to produce another message—one which may be similar to or different from the more obvious message being delivered by the speaker. To evaluate the entire communicative effort, the careful listener must consider certain aspects of the metamessage.

Combined with the aspects of nonverbal communication discussed in Chapter 1, the listener should compare relevant aspects of the formal message *with* what he knows of the *speaker* and of the *time, place, and circumstance* of *delivery*. If the speaker is personally recognized by the listener as a man of integrity, competence, and goodwill, it should be recognized that the message will probably "come over" encased in a predetermined atmosphere of acceptance. Right or wrong, most persons are influenced by the very nature of the people with whom they deal. In any walk of life, people are inclined to believe certain persons and to distrust others. From some, individuals are inclined to accept the biggest falsehood; from others, they are inclined to reject the most obvious truth.[3] Being aware of this tendency, in himself as well as in others, the responsible listener will try to identify the extent to which it has affected his evaluation of the message. He reminds himself repeatedly that no one is capable of creating masterpieces every time he works, regardless of his past reputation. Conversely, on occasion even the most ignorant person is capable of an irrefutable truth. The competent auditor tries to identify and separate *what* was said from *who* was saying it *at least until an evaluation on the basis of the relevance and validity of the ideas is completed*. This does not mean that it is always wrong to reject a message precisely because a particular speaker was presenting it. It does mean that each rejection for such a reason ought to be clearly identified so as to prevent the listener from believing his choice is based on more logical reasons. In sum, *the good listener forces himself to evaluate each message from each speaker on the basis of its merits*.

In addition, however, the sophisticated listener is responsible for noting the nature of the various metamessages sent out by the time, place, purpose, and mode of communication. He makes himself aware of the message revealed by the speaker's choice of *when* to communicate, to *whom*, and for *how long*.

The latest information drawn from the areas of psychology and psychiatry reminds us that very often the vocal and bodily actions we employ

---

3. S. C. Menefee, "The Effect of Stereotyped Words on Political Judgments," *American Sociological Review* 1 (1936), pp. 614-626.

or avoid employing reveal more about how we feel and what we think than the words we use. An alert earwitness recalls:

> . . . the obvious connections between bodily actions and illness, e.g., distorted facial expressions, involuntary movements (tics, blinking, twitches), uncoordinated movements of gait which accompany some states of health, abortive movements of stuttering. In less obvious instances, the habitual patterns of action, employed by the "normal" individual also reveal his state of mind. Random tapping, unrelated smiles, averted eye contact, constant shifting of weight, while they fall within the normal range of action, nevertheless convey meanings concerning basic personal adjustments to the world. In addition of course, such mobility, or non-mobility, connotes one's adjustment to the immediate situation.[4]

From all these things, the listener constructs the metamessage and compares it with the message itself to make his final judgment.

SUMMARY

To insure the success of his listening adventure, the auditor must become actively involved in the act of oral communication. He must focus his efforts on recording the speaker's message (and his metamessage) before he seeks to evaluate it. This recording is done best in writing but, regardless of how, it is most efficient and accurate when in outline form with special emphasis on the basic ideas. The recording as well as the evaluating process is helped by a discreet use of the art of questioning. The final process of evaluation includes a concern for the acceptability of the major ideas, the logical patterns employed to relate these ideas and the comparison of the message formed by these ideas with the metamessage given by the speaker as well as the time, place, and circumstances of delivery.

The careful listener crystallizes his participation by seeking answers to (1) What did he say? (2) What does he mean? (3) What is his degree of competence? (4) What is the nature and degree of his prejudice toward the subject?

The effective listener is guided by the truism, *"Audi et vivamus,"* or "Listen, and we shall survive."

PRACTICAL REMINDERS

Propositions
1. Effective listening includes distinct processes of recording and evaluating.

---

4. LaRusso, *op. cit.*, p. 223.

Skills of the Listener: Participation

2. Recording is best done in written, outline form, and whenever possible, makes use of the art of questioning:
   a. What did he say?
      1) Main ideas with relevant detail?
      2) Verbatim symbols not paraphrases?
      3) Listener's observations clearly marked?
   b. What did he mean?
      1) Did he speak irony, sarcasm, humor?
      2) Did he speak literally?
      3) Is there a metamessage?
3. Evaluating includes finding out:
   a. What is his degree of competence in the subject?
      1) Personal experience (training, education, work)?
      2) Nature and use of secondary sources (are they from competent experts, are they traditional, or are they common knowledge)?
   b. What is the nature and extent of his prejudice in this area?
      1) Is he a reluctant witness?
      2) Does he alter his known views for this occasion?

Exercises

1. How may the following questions be answered?
   a. Do you want to go?   b. Pardon me, please?   c. Would you mind passing the salt?   d. Don't you believe that ....?
2. What does the speaker mean by
   a. prewar   b. preschool   c. preshrunk   d. preheated
3. Have a friend observe your listening habits on several occasions of his own choosing when you are unaware of his observations. Compare your reaction to each speaking situation with his record of your activity. Does any pattern emerge?

Readings

Broadbent, Donald E. "Failures of Attention in Selective Listening." *Journal of Experimental Psychology* 44: 428-433, 1952.

Jastrow, Joseph, ed. *The Story of Human Error*. New York: D. Appleton-Century Co., 1936.

Johnson, Wendell. *People in Quandaries*. New York: Harper and Brothers, 1946.

Mason, Harry. "Personal Values as Factors in Listening Ability." *American Psychologist* 4: 395ff., 1949.

Reik, T. *Listening With the Third Ear*. New York: Farrar, Strauss & Company, 1948.

Weaver, Carl H. "Don't Look It Up—Listen!" *Speech Teacher* 6: 240-246, 1957.

INDEX

INDEX

Action, 23-7, 32-3, 98-101
Analogy, 72, 124
Attitude, 29-31, 121
Audience
  age range, 58
  analysis, 40-1, 56-61, 88-93
  capabilities, 39-42, 59, 115-17
  physical state, 58-9
  previous activity, 59
  psychological state, 59, 115-17
  purpose, 58
  seating, 75, 115-16
  size, 58, 90-1
  status, 59
Audiovisual, 104-7
Augustine, St., 11, 42
Authority, 74-5

Bacon, Francis, 98
Birdwhistell, Ray, 7
Bodily action, 23-7, 29, 32-3, 98-101
Bruner, Jerome, 23
Buber, Martin, 8, 44
Bulwer, John, 98

Calder, Nigel, 14
Campanella, Tommaso, 99
Cassirer, Ernst, 3, 4
Chomsky, Noam, 23
Clarity, 67-8
Competence, 52-6
Composition, 81-3
Conviction, 56
Cooper, Lane, 58
Cycle, 10

Deduction, 70-1
Delivery, 23-7, 94-108
Della Casa, Giovanni, 98

Depth, 11
Development, 70-8
Dianoia, 22

Ecclesiastes, 10
Elyot, Thomas, 98
Empathy, 99
Enthymeme, 71, 83, 85
Esar, Evan, 76
Ethics, 29, 30, 31, 42-5, 51
Experience, 52-3
Eyes, 25, 101

Fast, Julian, 25
Feedback, 60-1
Form, 20
Fuller, John, 76

Gesture, 25-6, 99-101
Gilkinson, 11, 74
Goodwill, 56
Grammar, 81
Griswold, A. Whitney, 28

Hollingsworth, H. L., 92
Homeostasis, 41, 51
Humor, 75-8, 84

Images, 15
Induction, 70, 71-2
Integrity, 50-2

Kant, Immanuel, 14

Language, 33-4, (See Style)
Lao-Tzu, 27
LaRusso, Dominic, 120, 126
Lewis, Thomas, 90
Libraries, 53-6

Linguistic Devices, 82-3, 87
Listening, 44, 111-127
Location, 90-1
Locke, John, 71
Logic (logical), 70-3, 123-25

Martin, Harold, 49
Maslow, Abraham, 23
McLuhan, Marshall, 20
Mead, George, 30
Meaning, 6, 27, 79-80, 119-21
Menefee, S. C., 125
Message, 67-87
Metaphor, 83
Models, ix, x
Montagu, Ashley, 26
Movement, 27

Nonverbal, 7-27
Note-taking, 53-6, 113, 119-20

O'Brien, Justin, 111
Order, (See Organization, Time), 9, 69-70
Organization, 9-10, 31-2, 40-1, 69-70
Overstreet, Harry, 44, 53

Parallelism, 83
Pei, Mario, 7
Perelman, Chaim, 22, 51
Persuasion, 31, 67, 71
Pfeiffer, John, 43
Pike, Kenneth, 7
Pitch, 102-3
Polanyi, Micheal, 7, 23
Posture, 24-5
Practice, ix-x, 96-8
Principle, 39-46, 52, 67, 94-6, 100, 103, 114
Pupillography, 25

Quality, 86
Questioning, 121-3

Rahskopf, Horace, 95
Rate, 102-3
Reason (See Logic, Induction, Deduction)
Rehearsal, (See Practice)
Research, (See Libraries)
Rhythm, 93, 11-12, 104
Riesman, David, 45
Rogers, Carl, 43, 115, 123

Silence, 111
Simile, 83, 86
Situation, 88-93, 101-2
Social Responsibility, 42-5, 111
Sommer, Robert, 18
Space, 14-19
Speaker, 50-6
Spitzer, H. F., 94
Stage Fright, 32
Style, ix, 78-83
Syllogism, 70-1, 124
Symbolization, 3, 4, 33-4
Symbols, 3-7, 113, 119, 125
Synapse, 8

Theme, 68-9
Theory, ix, x
Thought, 31-2, 122
Time, 8, 9-14, 46, 88-91, 113, 125
Touching, 26
Training, ix, x, 52-3
Transitions, 120-2, 124

Understatement, 83
Unfolding, 13

Verbal, 3-7, 27-35
Voice, 33, 101-4
Volume, 103-4, 120

White, William, 31
Woodrow, H., 96
Words, 79-80

Yacorzynski, G. K., 41